LEVITICUS
God Among His People

LEVITICUS
God Among His People

by
SAMUEL J. SCHULTZ

MOODY PRESS
CHICAGO

© 1983 by
THE MOODY BIBLE INSTITUTE
OF CHICAGO

All Scripture quotations in this book are from *The Holy Bible: New International Version,* © 1978 by the New York International Bible Society. Used by permission of Zondervan Bible Publishers.

Library of Congress Cataloging in Publication Data

Schultz, Samuel J.
  Leviticus: God among His people.

  (EBC)
  Bibliography: p. 141
  1. Bible. O.T. Leviticus—Commentaries. I. Title.
II. Series: Everyman's Bible commentary.
BS1255.3.S38   1983   222'.1307   83-19316
ISBN 0-8024-0247-X

4 5 6 7 Printing/EP/Year 92 91 90 89 88

Printed in the United States of America

CONTENTS

PREFACE

Leviticus may be the most neglected book in the Old Testament. Repeatedly the resolution to read the entire Bible from Genesis to Revelation has been abandoned when the reader has seen little relevance in the rituals and offerings prescribed under Moses.

But the message of Leviticus is vital to the God-man relationship delineated throughout the Bible. How can man approach a holy God? How can man maintain continued fellowship with the living God? For the Israelites, God's revelation in Leviticus provided guidance. Through faith and obedience to its precepts in everyday life, they had access into the presence of God.

The foundation of the book of Leviticus is God dwelling among His people. The Israelites had been miraculously freed from Egyptian slavery. During a one-year encampment at Mount Sinai, two important events occurred: the establishment of the covenant (Ex. 19-24) and the building of the Tabernacle as a dwelling place for God among His people (Ex. 25-40).

When the Tabernacle was completed and the prescribed sacrifices offered by Moses and Aaron, God manifested His presence in all His glory (Lev. 8-9). God was now residing among His people and the Tabernacle was their meeting place. How to maintain the vital covenantal relationship between the Israelites and their God is the concern of the book of Leviticus.

The uniqueness of God dwelling among His people stands out against the Israelites' cultural and religious context in Mosaic times. In contrast to the enneads of Egyptian gods and the pantheon of Canaanite gods, the Israelites had only one God. In contrast to the many temples in Egypt and the multiplicity of shrines in Canaan, the Israelites had just one sanctuary for worship.

Equally unique was the reality that the Israelites worshiped a living, active, all-powerful God who had vividly made them aware of His love and grace by delivering them from Egyptian enslavement. In contrast to worshipers who had to care for man-made idols, the Israelites had received manna from their God, which provided daily sustenance and providential care.

As a meeting place between God and His people, the Tabernacle could hardly be compared to the pagan shrines of other Near Eastern nations. The debasing practice of paganism, particularly in the Canaanite fertility cult, which involved sacred prostitution, stood in marked contrast to the ministration of holy priests at the Tabernacle. Whereas Anath, a principal goddess of the Canaanites called "the holy one" was a sacred prostitute, the God of Israel expected those who worshiped Him to show forth in their daily lives the spiritual and moral qualities of a truly holy God.

The relationship between God and man is unfolded in its fullness in the revelation of Jesus Christ. To the New Testament writers, the book of Leviticus was basic to an understanding of the Christian faith and doctrine. The book of Hebrews especially provides an enriching commentary on Leviticus, particularly in its emphasis on Jesus Christ as the one who makes man holy through His identification with the human race (e.g., 2:11).

I covet for the reader of this volume a fuller understanding of the holiness of God and His provision for human-divine fellowship. In the Tabernacle, and more fully through Jesus Christ, God has manifested Himself to man with the promise that He ever delights to dwell in the hearts of the humble and contrite (Isa. 57:15).

Outline

I. Introduction
　　Title and Place in the Pentateuch
　　Material of Leviticus

1

INTRODUCTION

TITLE AND PLACE IN THE PENTATEUCH

The third book of the Old Testament was identified among the Hebrew scrolls by its opening word, *wayyiqra,* "and he called." When it was translated into Greek (in the Septuagint) in the third century B.C., it was entitled *Leveitikon* or *Levitikon,* an adjective qualifying *Biblion* (book). The Latin version (Vulgate) centuries later was entitled *The Levitical,* from which our English title *Leviticus* is derived.

The Jews seemed to have a better designation for the scope of this book when in the Mishnah they called it the "priests' law," "priests' book," and "law of offerings." Later, in the Talmud, they designated it as "Law of the priests." The Syrian Christians called it in the Peshitta "the book of the priests."

Although this book deals largely with priestly matters, the Levites are mentioned only once (25:32-34), not in reference to ritual functions but with regard to conditions governing land tenure. A careful reading of the text indicates that the book was addressed to Moses, Aaron, the congregation of Israel, and the priests, to guide them in maintaining a vital relationship with God in matters of worship, religious celebrations, and holy living.

The book of Leviticus is essential to the Pentateuch. The history of Israel began with the establishment of a vital relationship between God and Abraham, delineated in God's covenantal promise to the patriarchs (Gen. 12-50). When God called Moses, His promise was renewed and confirmed

through His mighty acts in leading Israel out of Egypt
(Ex. 1-18). As the Israelites were encamped at Mount Sinai,
God established His covenant with them as a nation
(Ex. 19-24).

The Israelites camped at Mount Sinai approximately one
year, leaving under divine guidance on the twentieth day of
the second month of the second year after the Exodus (Num.
10:11). While at Mount Sinai, God gave to Israel through
Moses the most extensive revelation to be recorded in the Old
Testament. Consequently, approximately one third of the
Pentateuch (Ex. 19-40; Lev. 1-27; and Num. 1-10) relates to
Israel's religion and was revealed to them during that year at
Mount Sinai. Although most of the material in this part of the
Pentateuch is revelatory, several significant events carry the
historical narrative along.

1. Most significant was the establishment of God's covenant
   with Israel (Ex. 19-24). After that, Moses spent two forty-
   day periods on Mount Sinai. Most of the rest of that year
   was devoted to elaborate preparation, making the priestly
   garments and building the Tabernacle, with all its expensive furnishings (Ex. 25-39).
2. The Tabernacle was erected on the first day of the first
   month of the second year (Ex. 40) and dedicated as the
   dwelling place of God in the camp of Israel (cf. Num. 7-8).
3. The priesthood was instituted during an eight-day period
   (Lev. 8-10) in which the Tabernacle and its furnishings
   were dedicated (Ex. 40).
4. The Passover was observed on the fourteenth day of this
   month, marking the first anniversary of the Israelites' exodus from Egypt (Num. 9).
5. On the first day of the second month of the second year, a
   census was taken and Israel was organized, in preparation
   for her departure from Sinai on the twentieth day of that
   month (Num. 1-4).

The longest narrative segment in Leviticus, chapters 8-10,
describes the institution of the priesthood. That segment is a
very significant link in the Pentateuchal narrative and is basic

to an understanding of Israel's relationship with God.

<h2 style="text-align:center">THE MATERIAL OF LEVITICUS</h2>

The material of this book lends itself readily to the following divisions:

1. Instructions and laws on sacrifice (chaps. 1-7)
2. Institution of the priesthood (chaps. 8-10)
3. Treatment of uncleanness (chaps. 11-15)
4. The Day of Atonement (chap. 16)
5. Instructions for holy living (chaps. 17-27)

Leviticus has a larger percentage of material attributed to God as the speaker than any other book in the Bible. Repeatedly the statement "God said" or "God commanded" indicates that what follows was given by God to Israel. Moses was the key person to whom and through whom God communicated with His people. Frequently he was instructed to convey God's messages to Aaron, the priests, and to the whole assembly of Israel.

Following is a summary of the divine-human communication in Leviticus:

1. Nine times in chapters 1-7 it is stated that God spoke to Moses, giving instructions concerning sacrifices: God spoke to Moses (5:14; 6:1); God told Moses to speak to the Israelites (1:1; 4:1; 7:22, 28); God spoke to Moses with instructions for Aaron (6:8, 19, 24).
2. Chapters 8-10 state only twice that God spoke, once to Moses (8:1) and once to Aaron (10:8). However these chapters repeatedly say that what was being done was in accordance with what God had commanded, The material in 8:4, 5, 9, 13, 17, 21, 29, 34, 36 reflects the instructions previously given to Moses on Mount Sinai (Ex. 29). Leviticus 9:6, 7, 10, 21 seems to be a freer summary of the instructions in Leviticus 1-7; and 10:7, 13, 15 reflect instructions in chapters 6-7. Thus most of the material in chapters 8-10 originated with God's direct communication.
3. The instructions to Moses concerning uncleanness are

given in 12:1 (to be conveyed to Israel) and 14:1. Four
times God spoke to Moses and Aaron (11:1; 13:1; 14:33;
15:1).

4. The instructions in chapter 16 for observing the Day of
Atonement were spoken by God to Moses. The entire
chapter is headed by the words "the Lord spoke to
Moses," and Moses gave the instructions to Aaron.

5. Throughout the principles and instructions for holy living
(chaps. 17-27), the expression "the Lord spoke to Moses"
occurs seventeen times. Eleven sections tell of Moses' being directed to give each message to the Israelites (18:1;
19:1; 20:1; 23:1, 9, 23, 26; 24:1, 13; 25:1; 27:1). Two
messages were to be conveyed to Aaron (17:1 and 21:16)
and four to Aaron and his sons (21:1; 22:1, 17, 26). The
principles and instructions as a whole are considered to
have their origin in God.

In light of the above summary, it is obvious that most of
the content of Leviticus was revelation, communicated to the
Israelites through Moses, whom God chose to speak for Him.

WRITTEN FORM

When was the material in Leviticus committed to writing?
According to Exodus 19, the Ten Commandments were
spoken by God to the Israelites, but in subsequent days written copies were provided for the Israelites (Ex. 24:4;
34:27-28). After that, Moses addressed the whole Israelite
community, instructing it to build the Tabernacle as God had
commanded (Ex. 35:4-19). When were the instructions concerning the Tabernacle, the priesthood, offerings and observances (the revelations recorded in Exodus 25-31; 35-39;
Leviticus 1-27) committed to writing?

Since the turn of the twentieth century, Old Testament
scholarship has maintained that Leviticus, together with parts
of Genesis, Exodus and Numbers, constituted a literary docu-
ment composed in exilic times c. 550 B.C. That priestly docu-
ment (P), according to the classic exposition of Julius
Wellhausen, in his *Prolegomena to the History of Israel*

(1878), reflected a religious evolution in which the simple, spontaneous worship of early Israel had developed, by exilic times into a ritualistic legalism. That theory has dominated biblical scholarship for about a century and permeates commentaries, Bible dictionaries and encyclopedias, and textbooks. Even though the view is purely theoretical, it is accepted by modern, naturalistic scholarship as axiomatic and frequently is not subjected to critical examination.

When that theory was advanced by Wellhausen and his fellow scholars in the nineteenth century, relatively little was known about the cultural, literary, and religious customs of the second millennium .B.C., the time of Moses. The Wellhausen dictum that Moses could not write, and that writing before the time of David was limited to specialists, was advocated as late as 1893 (cf. H. Schultz, *Old Testament Theology,* 1:25). Since the turn of the century, archaeological excavations have provided extensive information concerning the cultural context of Old Testament times that necessitates an examination of some of the theories advocated decades ago.

Actually, writing dates back to about 3100 B.C. Egyptian and Akkadian literature has provided evidence of extensive literary interests in the Nile and Tigris-Euphrates centers of education as early as the middle of the third millennium B.C. Before 1929, very few texts of the West Semitic dialects, to which biblical Hebrew belongs, could be traced to earlier than 900 B.C., but the discovery of Ugarit (1929), a Northwest Semitic language quite closely related to Hebrew and Canaanite/Phoenician, gives evidence for its common use along the Mediterranean coast during the thirteenth-fourteenth century B.C. Excavations at Mari along the Euphrates (1930) date the use of the West Semitic dialects back to the eighteenth century B.C. Now the recent discovery of the Ebla-Mardikh literature points to an extensive use of the West Semitic dialects throughout the Kingdom of Ebla, about 2400 B.C.

Thus, significantly, the West Semitic dialects to which Hebrew belongs were in use in the heart of the Fertile Crescent about four centuries before the time of Abraham and approximately a thousand years before the Mosaic era. In the light of that historical and cultural background, it would seem quite appropriate to believe that Moses would have used the Hebrew language to record matters that he considered important for his people, Israel, to know as they settled in Canaan.[1]

In view of the priestly nature of the book of Leviticus, it is important, in considering Moses as author, to note the literary involvement of the priesthood in the ancient Near East.[2]

Early in the third millennium B.C., the Sumerians established the tradition of giving the priesthood responsibility for all forms of education. In major areas of concern, such as the cultus, medicine, civil administration, and law, the important procedural canons were usually committed to writing very early. Those were transmitted in written form by scribes and pupils, without editing or changes in the text. In Egypt, such literature as the "Pyramid texts," medical texts, and Memphite theology, which magnified deity Ptah as the First Cause, was written down in the third millennium B.C.

Scribal practice in the Near East indicates that commonly used liturgies and rituals were committed to writing and passed on for centuries and communicated to the people orally from the written copies. Priestly traditions related to the cultus were especially important and were preserved in writing for repeated usage.

No statement in the book of Leviticus ascribes authorship to Moses. In the book of Exodus certain sections are credited to him (17:14; 24:4; 34:27). The last two references tell of Moses' writing down the material revealed to him at Mount Sinai. Because the bulk of Leviticus was given through direct revelation, it seems logical that Moses would have been equal-

---

1. K. A. Kitchen, *The Bible in Its World* (Downers Grove, Ill.: Inter-Varsity, 1977), p. 49.
2. R. K. Harrison, *Introduction to the Old Testament* (Grand Rapids: Eerdmans, 1969), pp. 591-98.

ly concerned about preserving it for future generations and thus would have committed it to writing soon after communicating it orally to his people.

During the early years of his life, Moses had been educated in Egypt. In all likelihood he was familiar with, if not involved with, the literary activities of the Egyptian priests who were responsible for education. Since it was customary for the priesthood to commit religious rituals and medical and administrative instructions to writing, it is certainly probable that Moses would have done the same when he was responsible for those matters.

When the materials for building the Tabernacle were collected, Moses assigned the Levites, under the direction of Ithamar, son of Aaron, to make a record of the contributions (Ex. 28:21). It is thus reasonable to assume that Moses asked the Levites and priests also to record the instructions that God communicated to him on Mount Sinai, which may have involved them in research and the writing of the entire Pentateuch before Moses died.

Of particular interest is the literary form in Leviticus of the regulations concerning sacrifices (1:1—7:38). The purity of the Hebrew text in these chapters, which contain only minor difficulties, leads Harrison to conclude that this sacrificial legislation is "an original, unadulterated core of Hebrew" writing.[3] It was characteristic in ancient Near Eastern nations to exercise great care in transmitting priestly material in the exact form in which it had been written by the scribes.

The conclusion of that legislation (7:37-38) is written in a colophon form frequently used in ancient Mesopotamian documents. The colophon—often containing the title or designation, the date of writing, and the name of the owner or scribe—was usually the conclusion of a tablet. In the book of Genesis, eleven such literary units are identified by "these are the generations of." As was characteristic in a colophon, the

---

3. R. K. Harrison, *Leviticus* (Downers Grove, Ill.: Inter-Varsity, 1980), pp. 84-87.

material here is identified as commanded by God (cf. the title in 1:1) and given by Moses, the owner or scribe to whom God gave the regulations "on Mount Sinai on the day He commanded the Israelites to bring their offerings to the Lord, in the Desert of Sinai" (7:38).

Consequently, the material regulating sacrifices is regarded as authentic second-millennium literature. In content and form it is so similar to other literature of that period that it is reasonable to assign the authorship to Moses.

Moses may have been acquainted with quite a few languages of the Fertile Crescent. During the New Kingdom era, Egypt was the most powerful kingdom in the Near East, extending its conquest and control up to the Euphrates River and beyond. Most likely Moses was familiar with the Northwest Semitic language, which included the Eblaite, Hebrew, and other Canaanite languages such as Phoenician and Ugaritic (which used a local cuneiform alphabet). He may also have known the East Semitic (Sumero-Akkadian) common to the Tigris-Euphrates region.

Moses also had training in the history and religion of his forefathers, Abraham, Isaac, and Jacob, especially in regard to the promises God had made to Israel. Being personally involved with Israel's religion he was aware of its uniqueness in contrast to the religions of the Egyptians and Canaanites. Thus he had a basic concern that the Israelites carefully maintain a vital relationship with God. (That concern was later expressed in his oral communication to all Israel, recorded in Deuteronomy.) Consequently he would have been careful to preserve in writing the revelatory material entrusted to him to communicate to Israel. It would have been quite normal to write the revelations down soon after he had communicated them orally to the priests and the assembly of Israel.

Crucial to the question of when and by whom the book of Leviticus was written is an understanding of revelation and inspiration. Throughout the text, the statement that God spoke to Moses (and Aaron) occurs thirty-eight times. If that frequent assertion is accepted as trustworthy, then God communicated orally with Moses in giving His revelation. Does the modern scholar who accepts the standard critical view that Leviticus was written around 550 B.C. accept the material as divinely revealed to Moses? If so, then we may look for some documentation or evidence that the material was transmitted with accuracy for so many centuries after being revealed to Moses. Would inspiration or the guidance of the Holy Spirit ensure that what had been transmitted orally for such a long time would be recorded accurately?

From a human perspective it is reasonable to assume that the reliability of the account would correlate to the proximity in time between the first written copy and Moses himself, the recipient of divine revelation. If Moses had recorded the content of God's revelation without divine aid, the written copy would have been subject to error. If one recognizes with the New Testament writers that the Old Testament was written under the inspiration of the Holy Spirit, then the written text can be accepted as a trustworthy and reliable account of what God had revealed to Moses. It was, in fact, accepted as such in New Testament times.

So we see that the book of Leviticus is more than mere history or an ordinary manual for priests. In addition to Moses' historical, cultural, and religious context, one should recognize that *God spoke,* and Moses listened and communicated *God's revelation* to the Israelites, who had been miraculously delivered from Egyptian bondage. Since Moses had written other historical, legal, and revelatory material for his people, as indicated in Exodus, Numbers, and Deuteronomy, we can be confident that soon after his oral communication, the Leviticus material was committed to writing for future generations.

THEOLOGICAL CONTEXT

The narrative of Leviticus portrays Israel, an independent nation, in relationship with God. The book gives instructions for many aspects of everyday life, in which the Israelites were to reflect that they were God's holy people. Under the guidance of the priesthood, they were taught to maintain a right relationship with God through sacrifices and offerings. If the relationship was broken through sin, it could be restored through the proper offering. Observances of the feasts and seasons incorporated into their pattern of living a continual reminder that they were God's people.

To understand the content of Leviticus it is essential to consider the theological background of Israel as a nation. To bring Israel's theological setting into focus, let us consider the patriarchal promise, Israel's redemption out of Egypt, the covenantal agreement, the Tabernacle, and the priesthood.

THE PATRIARCHAL PROMISE

God's promise to Israel began with Abraham, through whose descendants all the nations of the earth were to be blessed (Gen. 12:1-3). With that promise came the assurance that in the future they would, as a nation, occupy the land of Canaan. As the Israelites under Joseph settled in Egypt, the hope of returning to the land promised to them was kept alive from generation to generation by an oath that the bones of Joseph would be transferred to Canaan when God fulfilled His promise to them (Gen. 50:22-26; cf. also Heb. 11:22).

Generations later, the Israelites were oppressed by the Egyptians in whose land they lived. Under enslavement and oppression, Moses was born, cared for and influenced by his mother, and reared and educated in the court of Pharaoh. Under his mother he undoubtedly became aware of the promises God had made to the patriarchs, and he chose to identify himself with his fellow Israelites instead of the Egyptians (Ex. 2:11-23; cf. Heb. 11:24-26). When God called Moses to deliver Israel, He identified Himself as the God of Abraham, Isaac, and Jacob and declared that He would fulfill His promise of bringing the Israelites into their own land (Ex. 3:6-9).

REDEMPTION OF ISRAEL

Although the enslaved Israelites had appealed to God for

help on the basis of the patriarchal promises, they had not
seen any evidence of divine power displayed on their behalf.
Instead they continued to live under oppressive Egyptian
pharaohs of the New Kingdom era, whose power was unchal-
lenged in the Fertile Crescent.

But God was concerned about their oppression (Ex.
2:23-25). In carrying out His plan to free the Israelites from
Egyptian oppression and to guide them to the Promised
Land, God involved Moses (Ex. 3:1-10). Through Moses God
provided the conditions and circumstances that gave the
Israelites a basis on which to exercise their faith in God.

How did God reveal himself to the Israelites? Moses anticipated that the Israelites would not believe that God had
appeared to him at the burning bush (Ex. 4:1), so God en-
dowed him with two miraculous signs. When the Israelites
saw those signs and accepted Moses and Aaron as messengers
of God, "they believed" and "bowed down and worshiped"
(Ex. 4:31).

God's power was subsequently demonstrated to the Israelites as well as to the Egyptians in the course of ten plagues.
God's power was displayed so that the Israelites would
"know that I am the LORD your God" by bringing them out
of Egypt (Ex. 6:7). The plagues were "mighty acts of judgment" so that the Egyptians would "know that I am the
LORD when I stretch out my hand against Egypt and bring the
Israelites out of it" (Ex. 7:4-5).

The final plague required the Israelites to observe the first
Passover celebration. Prepared for departure—"with your
cloak tucked into your belt, your sandals on your feet and
your staff in your hand"—they were to eat the Lord's
Passover feast (Ex. 12:11). Believing the instructions God
gave through Moses, the Israelites, under the leadership of
the elders, did as instructed and observed the Passover in an
attitude of worship and faith in God (Ex. 12:27-28; cf. Heb.
11:27-28).

As they left Egypt, God's presence with them was miraculously manifested in a "pillar of cloud to guide them" and

a "pillar of fire to give them light" (Ex. 13:20-22). When the
Israelites were endangered by the pursuing Egyptian army,
the pillar of cloud barred the enemy from overtaking them
(Ex. 14:19-20), and a way through the Red Sea miraculously
was made for the Israelites, whereas the Egyptians perished in
its waters.

As the Israelites witnessed God's mighty power displayed in
their redemption, they "feared the LORD and put their trust in
him and in Moses his servant" (Ex. 14:31). In that historic
deliverance the Israelites learned of God's loving concern for
their suffering as slaves of the powerful Egyptians. In contrast to the divine judgment meted out to the Egyptians, the
Israelites were favored by God's mercy and grace, through
which salvation was provided for them. Seeing the miraculous
signs, the Israelites responded in faith and obedience. They
learned to identify themselves as God's people, ones who
served a living, powerful God instead of the Egyptians.

THE COVENANT

En route to Mount Sinai the Israelites experienced God's
providential care. Water, manna, and quails were supplied in
abundance, and the attacking Amalekites were defeated.

At Mount Sinai the covenant between God and the Israelites, who already had a faith in God (Ex. 4:31; 14:31), was
established. God now reconfirmed His patriarchal covenant
with the nation of Israel (Ex. 19-24).

The covenant was established on the basis of God's love
and grace. It has the same literary form as other ancient Near
Eastern texts in which a suzerain imposed his terms and laws
on the vassal. Usually in suzerain-vassal treaties, the suzerain
made a treaty with the vassal whom he had conquered.[4] God,
however, did not conquer Israel. God extended His love for
the patriarchs to the Israelites and redeemed them from the

---

4. Meredith Kline, *Treaty of the Great King* (Grand Rapids: Eerdmans,
   1963); P. C. Craigie, *The Book of Deuteronomy* (Grand Rapids: Eerdmans, 1976), pp. 20-24.

power of Pharaoh (Deut. 7:7-8; 9:4-6). God's graciousness in this covenantal relationship was unique to the faith of Israel. God did not send Moses to the Israelites with the law and require them to accept it in order to be delivered from slavery. On the contrary, He redeemed Israel in an act of love and grace and brought her to Mount Sinai before the law was revealed to her. Note the law's opening words: "I am the LORD your God, who brought you out of Egypt, out of the land of slavery" (Ex. 20:2). God's grace and mercy preceded the law.

God's purpose in choosing and redeeming Israel as His "treasured possession" was that she would be "a kingdom of priests and a holy nation" (Ex. 19:5-6). The laws and stipulations He gave the Israelites were to help them live as His holy people. The Ten Commandments and the rest of the revelatory material in Exodus, Leviticus, and Numbers were a working out of the relationship between God and His people, who were to reflect His holiness in daily life.

Obedience to these laws and regulations was a normal response to God's love, and God assured the Israelites that He would continue "showing love to thousands who love me and keep my commandments" (Ex. 20:6). Keeping God's commandments required exclusive devotion to and worship of God. In Egypt, enneads of gods were worshiped, some dating back more than a thousand years. But God's people were to worship Him alone. The seriousness of rupturing the covenant of exclusive worship was demonstrated when severe judgment was meted out to the Israelites when they worshiped the golden calf (Ex. 32-33), after which the covenant was renewed.

To underline the graciousness of this covenant, we should emphasize that the Israelites were not God's covenant people because they obeyed the law. They had been God's people before the law was given. The instructions for holy living delineated in the book of Leviticus were prescribed for the Israelites so that they might know how to live as God's people.

As the recipients of God's redemptive love, the Israelites were to have an attitude of humility and gratitude and a sincere interest in conforming to God's laws out of love for Him. The legalistic conformity that later developed was a distortion of obedience in that it lacked the proper response of love.

THE TABERNACLE

The Tabernacle is central in a proper understanding of the material in Leviticus. It was the focal point of the sacrificial rituals, the institution and ministry of the priesthood, and various religious observances.[5]

After the covenant was confirmed on Mount Sinai (Ex. 19-24), God instructed Moses to "make a sanctuary for me, and I will dwell among them" (Ex. 25:8). In Egypt, the Israelites had been made aware of God's care for them through Moses' delivering His message, confirmed by two miracles (Ex. 4:29-31), and they were shown God's power through the plagues, which climaxed in their exodus from Egypt. The pillar of cloud was a visible manifestation of God's presence hovering over them as they left Egypt, and it guided them to Mount Sinai. With the covenant established, God's presence was to be more concretely portrayed by a Tabernacle in the midst of their camp.

In contrast to the Egyptians, who had built many temples, the Israelites were to erect only one place of worship. Whereas the Eyptians served and ministered to the gods they had made, the Israelites worshiped one God, the God who had demonstrated that He was more powerful than Pharaoh and all the gods of Egypt.

When the Tabernacle was completed and dedicated, it was covered by the cloud of God's presence and filled with His glory (Ex. 40:34-48). Through that cloud's hovering over the Tabernacle God provided guidance for encampment, and its

---

5. See Samuel J. Schultz, *The Old Testament Speaks,* 3d ed. (New York: Harper & Row, 1980), pp. 57-74 for a summary of Israel's religion.

movement provided guidance for the wilderness journey
(Num. 9:15-23; 10:33-34; Deut. 31:15).

In interpreting the rules and regulations for cleanliness in
everyday life, one should keep in mind the reality of God's
dwelling with Israel in the Tabernacle in the center of the
camp. The Israelites' behavior was to be constantly tempered
by the fact that they were in the presence of God.

The Tabernacle and later the Temple, which were dwelling
places for God, were ultimately destroyed, and the glory of
God departed. The apostle John, however, recognized centuries later that God was once more dwelling among men in
the Person of Jesus, who tabernacled, or "lived for a while
among us. We have seen his glory, the glory of the one and
only Son, who came from the Father, full of grace and truth"
(John. 1:14).

The Priesthood

For the Tabernacle to function as God's dwelling place in
the camp of Israel, it was essential to have individuals charged
with the responsibility of leading in the worship of God. For
that important aspect of Israel's religion, God instructed
Moses to ordain Aaron and his sons to serve as priests (Ex.
28:1; 29:44-46). The priests were to represent God before the
people and to represent the people before God in order to
maintain the covenant relationship between God and Israel.

References to priests who did not belong to the descendants
of Abraham are intriguing. In patriarchal times Melchizedek,
king of Salem, was identified as "priest of God Most High"
(Gen. 14:18). In Egypt Joseph married the daughter of the
priest of On (Gen. 41:45; 46:20). Priests who were landowners were given special recognition in Joseph's administrative policy (Gen. 47:22, 26). Moses married Zip-
porah, the daughter of Jethro, a Midianite priest who offered
sacrifices in praise to God for Israel's deliverance from Egypt
(Ex. 18:9-12). Before Mosaic times, offerings to God were
usually made by heads of families, as exemplified by Noah
(Gen. 8:20-21) and Abraham (Gen. 12:7; 13:4, 18; 22:1-13).

Very likely the priests in Israel until this time (Ex. 19:22) were heads of families, who, with the elders (Ex. 4:29), were responsible leaders who represented the Israelites in religious and civic affairs.

Moses' divine call to be a leader of Israel was confirmed through the Exodus. He represented God to the Israelites as well as to the Egyptians. He also represented the Israelites before God.

In the covenant established at Mount Sinai (Ex. 20-24), Moses was instructed to appoint Aaron, his sons Nadab and Abihu, and seventy elders to represent the Israelites in worship. Moses, however, also functioned as priest in building an altar, offering sacrifices, reading the Book of the Covenant to the Israelites, and sprinkling "the blood of the covenant" on the people as they made their commitment of obedience to God (Ex. 24:3-8).

After the covenant was ratified, God gave Moses detailed instructions for the erection of the Tabernacle as His dwelling place in the camp of Israel (Ex. 25-27). Aaron and his sons, as priests, were to be robed in elaborately prepared garments (Ex. 28-30). In a seven-day ceremony, the priesthood was to be instituted and consecrated, and the Tabernacle and all its furniture were to be dedicated as a dwelling place for God among His chosen people (Ex. 40:1-38).

Although the priesthood in Israel began with Moses (Ex. 24), it was Aaron and his sons who were given divine authority to be the priests in Israel (Ex. 28:1). Dressed in special official robes (Ex. 28:4-39, Lev. 8:7-9), Aaron was unique as the anointed high priest (Ex. 29:7), and when he died, the office was passed on to his son Eleazar (Num. 20:25-28). Because Aaron was a Levite, the Israelite priesthood resided in the tribe of Levi.

After the Israelites were redeemed out of Egypt, the firstborn son in every family was to be consecrated to God (Ex. 13:2; 22:29; 34:18-20), since they had been spared when the firstborn sons among the Egyptians were slain. During the year of encampment, a census was taken (Num. 2:32; cf. also

Ex. 38:26), and the Levites took the place of the firstborn sons as they ministered in the service of the sanctuary (Num. 3:5-13).

To understand the book of Leviticus properly, it is essential to realize how vital the role of the priests was in the life of Israel. Since Israel as a nation had a unique covenantal relationship with God, the priesthood and its ministrations were of the highest priority. The priests served as mediators, representatives between God and the Israelites, to preserve that unique divine-human relationship. Although the covenant relationship with God had been established through Moses' acting as mediator and priest, the Aaronic priesthood was charged with maintaining that covenant as a living reality in the life of the Israelites.

The priests were at all times to be conscious of God's presence in the Tabernacle. They represented a holy God in the midst of a nation that was to be holy. It was crucially important for them to exercise meticulous care in daily living a holy life.

THE PRESENCE OF GOD

The Israelites had become aware of God's presence in a new way in Egypt. For years they had suffered as slaves and prayed for deliverance as the Egyptian oppression intensified (Ex. 3:7-10). When Moses told the elders that God had commissioned him to lead the Israelites out of Egypt to the Promised Land and performed two miracles before them, they responded in faith (Ex. 4:29-31). They witnessed the mighty acts of God during the ten plagues, and then, while marching out of Egypt, they literally saw God's presence in the pillar of cloud by day and the pillar of fire by night (Ex. 13:21-22).

When the Egyptians were about to overtake them, God's visible presence in the cloud moved behind the Israelites and restrained the enemy forces. After the Israelites crossed the sea, in which the pursuing army was drowned, the Egyptians were made forcibly aware of God's presence, as God had assured Moses: "the Egyptians will know that I am the

LORD" (Ex. 14:4). The Israelites responded to the manifestation of God's presence with reverence and faith in God and in
Moses (Ex. 14:31).

En route to Mount Sinai the Israelites grumbled and were
again made aware of God's presence (Ex. 16:2-12). While
Aaron was speaking to the Israelites, the glory of God appeared, and the Lord spoke to Moses. In response to their
grumbling, God provided quail and manna so that "you will
know that I am the LORD your God" (v. 12).

It was at that time that the Sabbath was introduced to the
Israelites, to be observed. In response to God's material provision for them each day, with a double portion on the sixth
day and none on the seventh, they were to "bear in mind that
the LORD has given you the Sabbath" (16:29). The Lord
removed the necessity of gathering food on the seventh day
and instructed His people to observe it as a "day of rest, a
holy Sabbath to the LORD" (16:23). Thus the Israelites were
given every seventh day as a holy day in which they were to
acknowledge the Lord's presence in a special way.

At Rephidim, the Israelites lacked water and once more
questioned, "Is the LORD among us or not?" (Ex. 17:8). God
again confirmed His presence with them as Moses struck a
rock with his staff and tapped water in abundance for the
Israelites.

As the Israelites were encamped at Mount Sinai, God continued to make His presence visible in the cloud (Ex. 19:9).
Although He had already conveyed His message to the
Israelites through Moses (Ex. 19:3-8), He now spoke to Moses
from the cloud so that the people would "hear me speaking
with you and will always put their trust in you" (19:9). After
the Israelites had duly prepared themselves, God manifested
His presence through thunder and lightning "and a very loud
trumpet blast" so that "everyone in the camp trembled"
(19:16). As "smoke billowed up" and "the whole mountain
trembled violently" (v. 18), the Israelites heard the "voice of
God speaking out of fire" (Deut. 4:33). That meeting with
God culminated in the ratification of the covenant between

God and Israel (Ex. 20-24). Then Moses ascended the mountain as "the cloud covered it, and the glory of the LORD settled on Mount Sinai." To the encamped Israelites "the glory of the LORD looked like a consuming fire on top of the mountain" (Ex. 24:15-17). With the Israelites committed to be God's covenant people, the first instruction He gave to Moses on the mountaintop was for the Israelites to "make a sanctuary for me, and I will dwell among them" (Ex. 25:8).

When Moses returned from Mount Sinai after forty days, the Israelites had already broken their commitment to worship God exclusively (Ex. 32). Their defection was judged by a severe plague, in which thousands died, and God's presence was withdrawn from Israel. When Moses realized that, he appealed to God, pleading that it was futile for him to lead the Israelites to Canaan without God's presence (Ex. 33:12-16). Realizing that the uniqueness of Israel was God's presence with them, Moses asked to see the glory of God—a greater revelation of God than he had experienced so far. God not only granted that request but also gave Moses assurance of the renewal of the covenant with Israel. After another forty-day period on the mountain, Moses returned to the camp of Israel with a radiant face, reflecting the reality of having been in the presence of God (Ex. 34). Immediately the Israelites contributed gifts and labor toward building a dwelling place for God.

When the Tabernacle was completed, Moses was commanded to erect it and put all its furniture in place (Ex. 40:1-8). In a seven-day ceremony, as the presence of God hovered above it, the Tabernacle and all its furnishings were anointed with oil, dedicated, and set apart for God. Likewise, Aaron and his sons, as well as their priestly garments, were sanctified and set apart for serving God, as Moses officiated in offering daily sacrifices. On the eighth day, Aaron officiated and blessed the people, and then Moses and Aaron entered the Tabernacle. When they came out to bless the people again, "the glory of the LORD appeared to all the people. Fire came out from the presence of the LORD and consumed the burnt offering and the fat portions on the altar'' (Lev. 9:23-24). That fire, a miraculous manifestation of God, consumed the sacrifice, climaxing the initiation of the dwelling of God in the Tabernacle.

The concept of Deity residing among people in a portable shrine was familiar to Near Eastern nations in the fifteenth and fourteenth centuries B.C. It was normal for Egyptians to carry such a tent with them on military expenditions and erect it in the middle of the camp for worship. At that shrine, the leader was expected to obtain guidance and protection from the deity.

Unique to Israel, however, was the fact that their God, who had delivered them through His mighty acts, manifested His presence in fire and glory visible to the entire nation. Unique also was God's communication, witnessed by the Israelites, to Moses at Mount Sinai and at the Tabernacle. God's power, manifested in their deliverance from Egypt and daily provision of manna, and His presence in the Tabernacle assured them of the future supply of their spiritual and material needs, including the fulfillment of the promise that they would possess the land of Canaan.

The presence of God among His people is the key to understanding the book of Leviticus. God was present in every aspect of life, in the everyday mundane affairs as well as in religious concerns. God was living among them. The Tabernacle was His residence in Israel.

The sense of God's presence, which permeates the entire book, is indicated forty-two times by the expression "before the LORD." As the people brought their offerings and observed their feasts and seasons, they did it "before the LORD." Eleven times they were reminded that their offerings were to be a soothing "aroma" to the Lord, reflecting as it were the physical presence of God. In addition, they were reminded to "rejoice before the LORD" (Lev. 23:40).

The solemn statement "I am the LORD" occurs forty-six times throughout Leviticus, identifying Israel's God as the ever living, ever present One. Every aspect of daily life was af-

fected by the reality of the presence of God. Both the
Israelites and the Egyptians came to "know that I am the
LORD" in a tangible way. The Israelites experienced God's
mercy in redemption (Ex. 6:7); the Egyptians were confronted
with God's power in judgment (Ex. 7:4-5). Now the Israelites
were to apply the awareness of God's presence in everyday
life. Nothing in life, no matter how insignificant, could be
considered beyond God's presence with His people. The
presence of God among them was the basis for holiness and
holy living, and the book of Leviticus outlines the terms
under which true worship was accepted by God.

SUMMARY

For a meaningful understanding of the book of Leviticus,
one must consider its importance in the history of Israel.
Although the bulk of its contents consists of priestly laws and
instructions, the narrative section—chapters 8-10—provides a
vital historical link between the books of Exodus and
Numbers. Consequently those chapters are basic to our
understanding of Leviticus in its historical context.

The inauguration of the priesthood, as the Tabernacle was
dedicated as God's dwelling place in the camp of Israel, was
the climax of Israel's encampment at Mount Sinai. Fewer
than nine months had passed since they had arrived there (Ex.
19:1). After the covenant was established (Ex. 19-24), Moses
ascended the mountain for forty days and received instructions for the building of the Tabernacle and its furniture, for
making the priestly garments, for appointing the priesthood,
and for dedicating the Tabernacle as God's abode among His
people (Ex. 25-31). Crucial was the interlude in which Israel's
apostasy precipitated divine judgment (Ex. 32-33). It was
through Moses' intercession that divine judgment upon the
whole nation abated and the covenant bond was restored.
After another forty-day period on Mount Sinai, Moses
returned to supervise the building of the Tabernacle (Ex.
35-39), which was ready for erection on the first day of the
second year after their departure from Egypt. The building of

the Tabernacle and the institution of the priesthood confirmed Israel as God's holy people.

In view of the climactic significance of the building of the
Tabernacle, let us begin our study of Leviticus with chapters
8-10, as the framework in which to consider the priestly instructions in the rest of the book. Those instructions became
meaningful and significant to the Israelites only after the
Tabernacle had been erected and God actually began to live
among them. The priesthood was ordained to minister on
their behalf in the presence of God.

2

GOD AMONG HIS PEOPLE

LEVITICUS 8:1—10:20

For God to dwell among His people was unique in the culture of Mosaic times. In Egypt many temples had been built for the many gods that the Egyptians had made to worship. The Israelites very likely had seen those gods but never had seen them demonstrate any power in behalf of the Egyptians.

The Israelites had a living, active God, who had demonstrated His power in freeing them from Egyptian enslavement and in providing them sustenance and protection en route to Mount Sinai. There they had seen and "heard the voice of God speaking out of fire" so that they "might know that the LORD is God; beside him there is no other" (Deut. 4:32-38). This God communicated to them that He wanted them to construct a place in which He could dwell among His people.

Besides agreeing to the covenant between God and themselves, the most important thing the Israelites did at Mount Sinai was to construct the Tabernacle. Toward that goal, they voluntarily gave their gifts in abundance and devoted all their efforts. When Moses made his appeal for gifts, the people responded so liberally that their giving had to be restrained (Ex. 36:6-7). Involved in the actual construction of the Tabernacle were "Bezalel and Oholiab and every skilled person to whom the Lord had given ability and who was willing to come and do the work" (Ex. 36:2). Note that the "Spirit of God" was also active in the construction of the Tabernacle (Ex. 31:3; 35:31).

What happened during the week that the Tabernacle was dedicated is narrated in Exodus 40 and Leviticus 8-9. The accounts are complementary, and each would be incomplete without the other.

The account in Exodus 40 may be outlined thus:

Verses:

1-15   Instructions for Moses

    1-8   erect the Tabernacle with its furnishings

    9-11   anoint the Tabernacle with its furnishings

    12-15   robe and anoint Aaron and his sons for the priesthood

16-33   The Tabernacle prepared for God's dwelling

    16-19   the Tabernacle erected

    20-21   the Ark with Testimony in the Holy Place

    22-27   the table with bread, the lampstand, and the incense; altar in the forepart of the Tabernacle

    28-33   the altar of burnt offering and basin for washing in the court surrounding the Tabernacle

33-34   God's presence manifested

The account in Leviticus 9-10 supplements the Exodus narrative by describing how the instructions given to Moses for anointing the Tabernacle and the Aaronic priesthood (Ex. 40:9-15) were carried out. (Only the erection of the Tabernacle was reported in Exodus.)

Leviticus 8-9 may be outlined as follows:

Verses:

    8:1-3   Moses instructed to prepare for the anointing of Aaron and his sons

    4-5   Moses addresses the assembly of Israel before the Tabernacle

    6-9   Aaron robed in priestly garments

    10-11   The Tabernacle and furnishings anointed

    12   Aaron anointed

    13   Sons of Aaron robed

    14-17   Moses officiates at the sin offering, assisted by Aaron and his sons

    18-21   Moses officiates at the burnt offering

22-29   Moses officiates at the ordination offering
  30   Moses anoints Aaron and sons
  31   Instructions to Aaron and his sons to remain before the entrance of the Tabernacle seven days
9:1-6   Moses instructs Aaron before his sons, the elders, and assembly to offer the prescribed sacrifices so that the glory of the Lord will appear
7-11   Aaron offers the sin offering
12-14   Aaron offers the burnt offering
15-21   Offerings for the people
  22   Aaron blesses the people
23-24   Moses and Aaron enter the Tabernacle, return to bless the people, and the glory of the Lord is miraculously manifested

ORDINATION OF AARON AND HIS SONS (8:1-36)

After Moses had received instructions to build a Tabernacle (Ex. 25-28) he was told that Aaron and his sons should be appointed as priests (Ex. 29). Detailed prescriptions for the apparel of the high priest and instructions for the ceremonies dedicating the Tabernacle and the priests were also given to him on Mount Sinai. Note the divine assurance, "Then I will dwell among the Israelites and be their God. They will know that I am the LORD their God, who brought them out of Egypt so that I might dwell among them. I am the LORD their God" (Ex. 29:44-45).

With eager anticipation, the Israelites had devoted their efforts to the construction of the Tabernacle, its furniture, and the gorgeous garments for the priests. When this was completed Moses inspected their work, approved it, and blessed the people (Ex. 39:32-43). Now the great moment had come for God to take his abode with Israel.

Instructions (8:1-5). With the Tabernacle erected and all the furniture in place, Moses assembled the congregation before its entrance and shared with them God's instructions. Note Moses' role in dedicating the Tabernacle and instituting the priesthood. He was the mediator between God and Israel and officiated as priest in the ordination of Aaron and his sons. Even after Aaron was ordained, God seldom spoke to Aaron alone. Usually God spoke to him through Moses or in Moses' presence. It was God and Moses together who ordained Aaron to the high priesthood of Israel, Israel's most holy office.

That Aaron was ordained to the priesthood is significant. In the grave disruption of the covenant, when the Israelites made and worshiped the golden calf, Aaron had been a willing accessory (Ex. 32-33). Although Aaron had been chosen before that to be the high priest, it was through Moses' intercession (Ex. 28:1), that Aaron and the Israelites were spared from destruction by God's wrath. Aaron's being publicly presented to Israel as high priest demonstrated the greatness of God's forgiveness and grace, in that even a sinner like he could be used by God in the highest religious office. (Jesus demonstrated the same grace and forgiveness toward Peter, who had denied Him three times [John 21:15-19].)

Washing and robing (8:6-9). Distinctive apparel for Aaron and his sons had been made according to the instructions God had given Moses (Ex. 29-39). Washing with water, as God had prescribed (Ex. 29:4), was essential before robing. For this a basin was placed in the court surrounding the Tabernacle, between the altar of burnt offering and the Tabernacle entrance. Note that the ordinance for priests to wash their hands and feet before they ministered before the Lord at the altar was a lasting one (Ex. 30:17-21). That outward cleansing—clean hands—represented the need for an inner spiritual cleansing—clean heart (cf. Ps. 24:4; 73:13; Isa. 1:16).

Aaron's tunic was a long, sleeveless undergarment made of fine linen and embroidered and tied around the waist with a sash. Ordinary priests wore the same kind of undergarment (Ex. 28:39-41; 39:27-29). The cape or robe specifically for the high priest (Ex. 28:31-34; 39:22-26) was worn over the tunic and extended from the neck to below the knees. Over the cape

Aaron wore the ephod, two pieces of richly embroidered linen joined with shoulder straps and held in place at the hips by a waistband (Ex. 28:6-14). The most significant and mysterious part of the high priest's apparel was the breastplate (Ex. 28:15-30). Linked by a chain of pure gold to the shoulder strap of the ephod, it contained twelve stones engraved in gold with the names of the twelve tribes of Israel, a visible reminder that Aaron represented the Israelites before God. In the fold of the breastpiece were placed the Urim and Thummin (Hebrew words meaning light and perfection), which apparently were sacred objects used for casting lots. Although they provided the means for discerning the will of God, little is known about their function or the procedure used by the officiating priest.

The turban, or headdress, a close-fitting bonnet made of blue material, was both impressive and significant. Attached to that bonnet and extending across the forehead was a plate of pure gold, with the inscription "Holiness to the LORD." It served as a constant reminder that the essence of God's nature is holiness.

Anointing by Moses (8:10-13). In accordance with divine instructions (Ex. 40:9-11), Moses anointed the Tabernacle and all its furniture with an oil prepared especially for that purpose and no other (Ex. 30:22-33). It was used here with the divine assurance that its application would signify cleansing, consecration, or sanctification for holy service. Those material objects, the Tabernacle and its furniture that the people had constructed, were now made holy for the use of their God. The oil was applied seven times to the basin and to the altar, making the people keenly conscious of being in the presence of a holy God.

Moses anointed Aaron before the assembly. Pouring oil on Aaron's head, Moses consecrated him to minister as the high priest in Israel. (In later times, Samuel used oil to anoint Saul and David as kings of Israel, designating them as God-appointed rulers [1 Sam. 10:1; 16:13].) Having anointed

Aaron as high priest, Moses presented the tunic-clad sons of Aaron as assistants, as the Lord had commanded him.

Sin offering for purification (8:14-17). Moses officiated in presenting a sin offering for Aaron and his sons (Ex. 29:10-14), making atonement for them. The blood of the offering was also applied to the horns of the altar "to purify the altar." In that way Aaron and his sons, as well as the altar, were purified from any sins that might affect their service and mar their fellowship with God.

Burnt offering for dedication (8:18-21). After expiation for Aaron and his sons had been provided through the sin offering, Moses presented a ram for a burnt offering. Aaron and his sons laid their hands on the animal, acknowledging that that ram was their substitute. Moses then slaughtered the ram and sprinkled its blood on all four sides of the altar. In this offering the entire animal was burnt on the altar; its perishable elements became ashes as its true essence ascended as a sweet-smelling aroma pleasing to God. It thus represented the offerer's complete surrender and dedication to God for service.

Peace offering for ordination (8:22-30). With the peace offering for ordination, Aaron and his sons were inducted into the service of Israel's priesthood. Significantly, in this ordination ceremony Moses applied the ram's blood to the lobes of the right ears, the thumbs of the right hands, and the big toes of the right feet of Aaron and each of his sons. Applying blood to those bodily extremities represented the priests' total consecration in hearing the commandments of God and serving as His representatives before the people. In this offering the fat portions and the right thigh of the ram, a cake of bread, and a wafer were waved before the Lord by Aaron and his sons as a wave offering. Then the wave offering was completely burned on the altar as an ordination offering. Moses then waved the breast of the ram, which was his share of the offering, as his wave offering before the Lord, symbolizing his dedication.

Finally Moses sprinkled some of the anointing oil and some of the ram's blood on Aaron and his sons and on each of their garments. As Israel had become the people of God when the blood was sprinkled on her in the covenant ceremony (Ex. 24:1-8), so Aaron and his sons were visibly set apart, through the application of the blood, as God's special representatives among the people.

Seven-Day ordination (8:31-36). After the sacrifices were concluded, Aaron and his sons were to prepare a meal at the entrance of the Tabernacle. They prepared the breast of the ordination ram for Moses and the rest of the ram, with the exception of the fat parts and the right shoulder, for themselves. Then they all partook of the sacrificial meal together. Any remains of the unleavened bread and meat were burned up as the day ended.

That ceremony was repeated for seven days. Every day a bull was offered (Ex. 29:35). Although not explicitly stated, it is quite likely that the entire ritual was repeated each day. Aaron and his sons were freed from all secular involvement and devoted each day to God as they were dedicated and consecrated before the assembly that was gathered to witness the ceremonies at the entrance of the Tabernacle.

"To make atonement for you" (v. 34) expresses the purpose of those days of ordination and consecration. Aaron and his sons needed offerings to atone for their sins and to purify them for service in the presence of Israel's holy God. Those offerings for sins had to be repeated again and again as the high priest represented the people before God in the Tabernacle. The book of Hebrews emphasizes the contrast to Jesus, the High Priest who made an offering once for all (see, e.g., Heb. 9:27-28).

AARON CONFIRMED AS HIGH PRIEST (9:1-24)

Under Moses' supervision, during the seven-day ritual of

instituting the priesthood, Aaron was approved as high priest before the Israelite assembly. On the eighth day Aaron, assisted by his sons, began his service as high priest.

Instructions through Moses (9:1-7). Although Moses was not to serve as the high priest of Israel, he was the prophetic mediator through whom God's covenant relationship with Israel as a nation had been established. Now, before the Israelite assembly, Moses gave Aaron God's instructions for his initiatory service.

The offerings to be offered on this day were, for Aaron, a bull for a sin offering and a ram for a burnt offering; and for Israel, a male goat for a sin offering, a calf and a lamb for a burnt offering, a cow and a ram for a fellowship or peace offering, and a cereal or grain offering mixed with oil.

The purpose of the offerings was to make atonement for Aaron himself and for the people of Israel (v. 7), "so that the glory of the LORD may appear to you" (v. 6).

Offering for Aaron (9:8-14). Assisted by his sons, Aaron slaughtered the calf for his sin offering. Dipping his finger in the blood, he purified the horns of the altar of sacrifice in the Tabernacle court. On the altar he burned the fat, kidneys, and the liver covering as a sin offering for himself. The flesh and hide were burned up outside the camp.

Thus Aaron's initial act of service as high priest was to offer a sin sacrifice to make atonement for himself. Through that act of worship he acknowledged before all Israel his own need for atonement before coming into the presence of God in behalf of his people.

The offering of a calf may have reminded the Israelites, as well as Aaron, of the golden calf they had made and worshiped while Moses was on Mount Sinai (Ex. 32). Severe judgment had followed that great apostasy. Now by means of this calf offering, in accordance with divine instructions, atonement was provided for Aaron as he ministered before the entrance of the Tabernacle the Israelites had erected as God's dwelling place among them.

Aaron then sacrificed a ram as a burnt offering for himself. Again the blood was applied to the altar for purification. The entire ram, piece by piece, was consumed on the altar.

Offerings for the people (9:15-21). Having made atonement for himself, Aaron now officiated as high priest for his people. First he offered a goat as a purification offering. Then followed the burnt offering, in which a calf and a lamb were sacrificed, which was supplemented with a cereal or grain offering. The peace, or fellowship, offering that came next consisted of a cow and a ram.

Those offerings were not to atone for specific sins of individuals but to atone for the general sinfulness of the nation as a whole. They also expressed the nation's thankfulness and dedication to God and provided an opportunity for fellowship between the Israelites and God as Aaron mediated.

Divine confirmation (9:22-24). When Aaron finished offering the sacrifices for the people, he extended his hand toward the people in blessing before he stepped down. Although the blessing is not recorded here, it may have been the same as or similar to the one given in Numbers 6:23-24:

> The LORD bless you and keep you;
> The LORD make his face shine upon you
> and be gracious to you;
> The LORD turn his face toward you
> and give you peace.

Moses then joined Aaron in entering the Tabernacle. For Moses and Aaron, that must have been a most solemn moment of expectancy, as they anticipated the manifestation of God's glory. For this purpose they had meticulously carried out all the instructions for dedicating the Tabernacle and instituting the priesthood. When Moses and Aaron returned, they blessed the people, and God's glory appeared.

The glory of the Lord had not appeared over the Tabernacle during the seven-day period when the Tabernacle with all its utensils, and Aaron, his sons, and their garments had been anointed by Moses. In fact, months had passed since the Israelites had seen a manifestation of the glory of God. After the Israelites' apostasy in worshiping "gods of gold" under the leadership of Aaron, they were subject to God's judgment (Ex. 32-34), which had been restrained through Moses' intercession. Moses had then returned to Mount Sinai, where he saw the glory of God, and had returned with a radiance on his face that reflected his having spoken with God (Ex. 34:30). In that context, Moses had involved the Israelites in building the Tabernacle (Ex. 35-39). Before the building of the Tabernacle, the manifestation of God's glory apparently had been limited to the "tent of meeting" where Moses communed with God from time to time (Ex. 33:7-11; 34:29-35).

To encourage the Israelites in building the Tabernacle Moses may have reminded them of the promise that God had made regarding its purpose: "Then have them make a sanctuary for me, and I will dwell among them" (Ex. 25:8). The Israelites had also been assured that the Tabernacle with its utensils, as well as Aaron and his sons, would be consecrated by God. Note the explicit promise: "So I will consecrate the tent of meeting and the altar and will consecrate Aaron and his sons to serve me as priests. Then I will dwell among the Israelites and be their God" (Ex. 29:44-45).

Aaron's instructions on the eighth day were to make atonement for himself and for the people "so that the glory of the LORD may appear to you" (Lev. 9:6). The focal point was the altar of burnt offering, where Aaron had made the sacrifices. That large altar, three cubits high and five cubits square (c. 4.5 feet by 7.5 feet by 7.5 feet), which the Israelites had constructed according to the directions given through Moses (Ex. 27:1-8; 38:1-7), was designated as the particular place where every Israelite would be able to meet with God. Note the divine promise: "For the generations to come this burnt offering is to be made regularly at the entrance to the Tent of

Meeting before the LORD. There I will meet you and speak to you; there also I will meet with the Israelites, and the place will be consecrated by my glory'' (Ex. 29:42-43).

The climactic and perhaps the most awesome moment for Moses, Aaron, and the Israelites at Mount Sinai was this moment, when fire miraculously consumed the remains of the burnt offering on the altar. That manifestation of God's glory confirmed that God was indeed meeting with His people. Aaron had been accepted by God as the high priest of Israel. It was a unique and historic moment for the nation of Israel.

The glory of the Lord was also visible in the cloud that covered and ''filled the tabernacle'' so that even Moses could not enter it (Ex. 40:34-35). The Israelites' God, who had established a covenant with them, was now dwelling with them as He had promised in the Tabernacle they had erected. ''Then I will dwell among the Israelites and be their God. They will know that I am the LORD their God, who brought them out of Egypt so that I might dwell among them. I am the LORD their God'' (Ex. 29:45-46).

Both of those manifestations of God's glory were witnessed by the people, and they responded with a shout of joy and reverence.

Historically, that was the first time God had dwelt among the human race in a tabernacle. It occurred in the camp of the Israelites, who had been redeemed from enslavement and were chosen to be God's holy people, through whom all mankind was to be blessed.

The Tabernacle, later located in Shiloh, ceased to be God's dwelling place when the Ark was taken by the Philistines. The Israelites recognized then that the glory of God had departed (1 Sam. 4:21-22). Years later, when the Temple was completed, the Israelites again witnessed the manifestation of God's glory at the dedication ceremonies (2 Chron. 7:1-6).

In subsequent centuries, prophet after prophet warned the Israelites to abandon their apostasy. The Temple would be destroyed if in their daily pattern of living they did not acknowledge the presence of God among them (see, e.g., Isa. 1-6). Jeremiah warned that the Temple, God's dwelling place among them, would not in itself save Jerusalem from destruction (Jer. 7). Ezekiel vividly foretold the withdrawal of God's presence and glory from the Temple and Jerusalem (Ezek. 8-11) and their abandonment to destruction, which was fulfilled by the Babylonians in 586 B.C.

The Temple was eventually rebuilt, but the Israelites waited for centuries for the fulfillment of the promise that God would "come to his temple" (Mal. 3:1). Even though the glory of God was manifested at the announcement of Jesus' birth (Luke 2), Jesus was recognized by relatively few Israelites. John bore witness that the Word, which was God, "lived for a while among us. We have seen his glory" (John 1:1, 14). Following Jesus' death and resurrection, on the day of Pentecost, God's glory was manifested as the Holy Spirit came upon Jesus' followers and they received the gift of His indwelling presence in their lives.

DIVINE JUDGMENT (10:1-20)

The manifestation of the glory of God was the climactic event of Aaron's inauguration as high priest of Israel. Although the pillar of cloud displaying God's glory had appeared to the people of Israel as they left Egypt and had been visible at various times during that year of encampment at Mount Sinai, the manifestation of God's glory in igniting the remains of the sacrifice on the altar was unique.

But the triumph of God dwelling with Israel was followed, that same day, by tragedy. It was a solemn and sobering event for Aaron, the high priest of Israel.

Death of Nadab and Abihu (10:1-7). The exact nature of the sin of Nadab and Abihu, for which they were so swiftly judged, is not revealed. Scripture simply states, "They offered unauthorized fire before the LORD, contrary to his command" (v. 1). Now the fire, which moments earlier had come from the presence of the Lord to confirm His dwelling among the Israelites (9:24), came in judgment to consume the lives (although not the bodies) of Nadab and Abihu. This took place in the courtyard, near the altar, and their bodies were removed "away from the front of the sanctuary" (10:4) by two cousins, Mishael and Elzaphan, at Moses' command.

Moses, who had been involved in the inauguration ceremonies only in the concluding blessing, now had a word from the Lord for Aaron (v. 3):

> Among those who approach me
> I will show myself holy;
> in the sight of all the people
> I will be honored.

Nadab and Abihu evidently had not properly considered God's honor and holiness. During the preceding week they had been anointed and consecrated as assistants to Aaron. But in using "unauthorized fire before the LORD," on their own initiative and "contrary to his command," they failed to live up to their stewardship of responsibility to the Lord. Representing the people before God, they should have been exemplary in their spiritual sensitivity in serving the holy God now dwelling among them.

In response to Moses' words, "Aaron remained silent." He silently submitted to the righteous judgment of God in the taking of two of his sons, as their bodies were removed, still in their tunics, from the camp of Israel.

The two other sons, Eleazar and Ithamar, and Aaron were instructed by Moses to remain at the entrance of the Tabernacle or "you will die, because the LORD's anointing oil is on you" (v. 7). Untidy hair, torn clothes, and other signs of mourning were not permitted them; they were to be exclusively devoted to serve God as priests. Their relatives and the rest of the Israelites continued mourning as Aaron and his two remaining sons stayed at the Tabernacle to carry on their ministry. An interesting parallel is Jesus' demand for the exclusive devotion of his followers, even in the event of funerals (Matt. 8:21-22; Luke 9:59-60; 14:26-27).

God's word to Aaron (10:8-11). God then spoke directly to Aaron, forbidding him and his sons "to drink wine or other fermented drink whenever you go into the Tent of Meeting, or you will die" (v. 9). When they were on duty at the Tabernacle they were to abstain totally from strong drink.

The priests were responsible for teaching the Israelites all the laws given through Moses. With them rested the responsibility of distinguishing between the holy and the profane. Such matters required the use of their best intellectual abilities. Because of their accountability to God, they were not to risk the error that might result from their minds being dulled by wine.

The text does not state whether or not Nadab and Abihu had been guilty of "drinking wine or fermented drink," but some commentators have inferred that, since the prohibition against drinking was given to Aaron and his sons on this occasion.[1]

Offering regulations (10:12-20). Following the offerings (9:16-21), the priests were to have partaken of a meal of their share of the grain offering and the right thigh and the breast of the animal brought for the fellowship offering (Lev. 7:28-36). After God's judgment on Nadab and Abihu, Moses reminded Aaron and his two remaining sons to eat their allotted parts of the offerings. When Moses learned that Eleazar and Ithamar had burned their part of the sin offering outside the camp, he rebuked them in anger.

Aaron however intervened and appealed to Moses. He solemnly questioned whether God would have been pleased with his eating his part of the sin offering. Aaron had carefully offered the sin and burnt offerings for himself and his four sons earlier that day, in assuming responsibility as the Israelites' high priest (9:8-14). Those offerings had been followed im-

---

1. For example, Gordon J. Wenham, *The Book of Leviticus* (Grand Rapids: Eerdmans, 1979), p. 158.

mediately by offerings for the people, after which the glory of the Lord had appeared in a climactic and historic manifestation.

Aaron must have been shocked by the judgment that followed in the wake of that dramatic display of the presence of God. Very likely Nadab and Abihu had brought "unauthorized fire" without consulting Aaron. Consequently, their deaths had been entirely unexpected. Aaron was sobered by the manifestation of God's presence in judgment. Given the circumstances, it is understandable that Aaron and his two remaining sons did not eat the "holy things" allotted to them from the sin offering at this time.

"When Moses heard this, he was satisfied" (v. 20). He had nothing to say to criticize Aaron for his actions.

The manifestation of God's presence to Israel under Moses and to the crowd assembled on Pentecost at Jerusalem under the apostles may be compared in several ways. God's manifestation of glory to the Israelites was a unique historical event, repeated only when the Temple was dedicated under Solomon (1 Kings 8:10-12; 2 Chron. 7:1-6). In the New Testament manifestation of God's presence on the day of Pentecost, the focal point was not the Temple but the individuals who received the Holy Spirit of God. Whereas God had promised the Israelites that He would dwell among them in the Tabernacle (Ex. 29:44-46), Jesus, who was God dwelling among men, had promised the coming of the Holy Spirit to dwell in the hearts of those who loved and obeyed Him (John 14:15-23), which was fulfilled on the day of Pentecost (Acts 2:33).

Centuries earlier, the prophet Isaiah had foretold that personal relationship between God and man and had proclaimed God's promise to dwell in the hearts of the humble and contrite (57:15). The glory of the Lord is the protection of individuals who show love and compassion toward their fellow men (58:8-9). God is not primarily interested in dwelling in buildings but is vitally concerned with the individual "who is humble and contrite and trembles at my word" (66:1-2).[2]

Each manifestation of God's presence was followed by divine judgment resulting in the death of two people, Nadab and Abihu (Lev. 10:2) and Ananias and Sapphira (Acts 5:1-11). Nadab and Abihu were judged for bringing unauthorized fire, and Ananias and Sapphira for deception and misrepresenting themselves and their gift before God and the public. The swiftness of God's judgment conveyed the certainty of His awesome presence to those involved.

Peter, in his first epistle, reminds his readers that divine judgment begins in God's family (4:17). God has higher standards for those to whom He has revealed Himself. The nation of Israel was subject to curses and blessings (Lev. 26; Deut. 28) and was judged more severely than the surrounding nations (see, e.g., Amos 1-2). Even Moses himself was not allowed to enter Canaan because he "did not trust in me enough to honor me as holy in the sight of all the Israelites" (Num. 20:12). Later, an unnamed prophet died for his disobedience (1 Kings 13). King Uzziah, for his presumptuousness, was smitten with leprosy (2 Chron. 26:16-21), as was Gehazi, Elisha's servant, for his greed (2 Kings 5:20-27). The death of Aaron's sons conveyed the message that God's honor had been ignored by two of those who had been entrusted with priestly responsibilities.

---

2. Cf. Samuel J. Schultz, *The Gospel of Moses* (Chicago: Moody, 1974), pp. 126-27.

3

WORSHIP OFFERINGS
AND SACRIFICES

Leviticus 1:1—7:38

Offerings were a vital part of Israel's maintaining a right relationship with God. Once the Tabernacle was dedicated and the priesthood inaugurated, bringing offerings became part of Israel's daily worship as a nation. The priests had the responsibility of instructing the people and officiating at the sacrifices in accordance with the instructions given at Mount Sinai. The opening chapters of Leviticus detail the kinds of offerings that the Israelites were to bring on various occasions.

Why were the offerings so significant to Israel's worship and relationship with God? God had identified the Israelites as "my people" (Ex. 3:7) when He had called Moses to deliver them from Egypt. God had commanded Pharaoh to release Israel, God's "firstborn son . . . so that he may worship me" (Ex. 4:22-23). As Moses and Aaron confronted Pharaoh, they repeatedly raised the issue of worship as the basis of the directive to release the Israelites (Ex. 7:16; 8:1, 20; 9:1, 13; 10:7-10), and Pharaoh acknowledged that sacrifice was necessary to Israel's worship of God (Ex. 8:25-28). All the Israelites—men, women, and children, with their flocks and herds (Ex. 10:7-11; 12:31)—were to be free to "worship God in the desert" (Ex. 7:16), which included bringing offerings to God (Ex. 10:25-26). Thus, offering sacrifices was vitally important to the Israelites' relationship with God from the very outset.

The offering through which the Israelites experienced redemption or salvation was the sacrifice of the Passover lamb (Ex. 12:1-28), which was offered on the night of their departure from Egypt. It was through the blood of that sacrificial lamb that they were spared from the judgment of God upon Egypt. For that sacrifice there had been no altar. The lamb's blood had been applied to the top and both sides of the door frame of each home. Those who, in obedience to God, applied the blood were spared when God executed "judgment on all the gods of Egypt" (v. 12). In that crucial experience, the Israelites became palpably aware that it was through the application of blood that their lives were spared.

Although the word *atonement* does not occur in the account of the Passover experience, the Israelites were conscious of the vital importance of the blood in their redemption from Egypt. Later at Mount Sinai, the blood from the prescribed offerings was sprinkled on the altar and on the Israelites as the covenant between themselves and God was confirmed (Ex. 24:4-8). The instructions for ordaining the priests to officiate at the offerings (Ex. 29:36-37) indicated that it was through the blood that cleansing was made for the altar as well as the people in their approach to God (cf. Lev. 17:11).

Faith was vital to Israel's redemption from Egypt. The elders of Israel, after they heard God's message and witnessed divine confirmation through miracles, believed and worshiped (Ex. 4:31). When their faith was put into practice and they obeyed in applying the blood of the Passover lamb, they, with their families, were miraculously delivered from Egyptian bondage. As they marched out of Egypt and saw further manifestations of God's mighty power in protecting them, they "put their trust in him and in Moses his servant" (Ex. 14:31).

The elders again demonstrated faith when Moses communicated to them at Mount Sinai that they were to be "a kingdom of priests and a holy nation" (Ex. 19:1-9). In a commitment of obedience, they responded, "We will do everything the LORD has said." When God spoke to Moses, the Israelites heard His voice so that they would "always put their trust in you [Moses]" (v. 9).

Having been redeemed out of Egypt and responding in faith and obedience, the Israelites now were to be consecrated or sanctified (to "stay pure," in the new translation of the Torah[1]) in preparation for the ratifying of the covenant between God and Israel (Ex. 19:10, 14).

The following elements were basic to the relationship between God and Israel:

1. God would show His love "to thousands who love me and keep my commandments," but divine judgment awaited "those who hate me" (Ex. 20:5-6).
2. The Israelites were to offer burnt and fellowship offerings on an altar they were to build.
3. They were to be God's "holy people" (Ex. 22:31) in all civic and social relationships and were to beware of being ensnared in worship of the gods of the inhabitants of Canaan, whose land they were to possess.

The terms of the covenant were communicated to the Israelites and recorded by Moses (Ex. 24:3-4). The next morning they built an altar and offered burnt and fellowship offerings. Moses sprinkled the blood of the sacrificial animals on the altar and on the people as "the blood of the covenant" (Ex. 24:3-8). In response the Israelites vowed, "We will do everything the LORD has said; we will obey."

After the Tabernacle was completed according to God's instructions, sin and burnt offerings were offered in dedicating the Tabernacle and sanctifying Aaron and his sons for the priesthood. Then Aaron began his service as high priest of Israel, offering sin and burnt offerings for himself and for the nation (Lev. 8-9). The priests were charged with the responsibility of teaching the people and officiating in offering sacrifices for the nation as well as for individuals.

---

1. *The Torah* (Philadelphia: Jewish Publication Soc., 1962).

THE BURNT OFFERING (1:1-17; 6:8-13)

The burnt offering was the most common sacrifice. The priests offered it morning and evening of each day, on behalf of the entire nation.

In the biblical record, Noah was the first to offer a burnt offering (Gen. 8:20). After he and his family had been divinely spared from God's judgment on the rest of the human race, Noah built an altar and sacrificed a burnt offering. It was a "pleasing aroma" to God, so soothing that God assured Noah,

> As long as the earth endures
> seedtime and harvest,
> cold and heat,
> summer and winter,
> day and night,
> will never cease.
>   (Gen. 8:22)

That offering was apparently a natural expression of Noah's relationship with God. After that offering, God established a covenant with Noah.

Later, Abraham was commanded to give a burnt offering and actually sacrificed a ram (Gen. 22:2, 13). He thus maintained his relationship with God through his personal faith in and obedience to God (Gen. 22:15-16). After that experience, Abraham was reassured of God's covenant with him.

The focal issue in the Levitical regulations concerning sacrifice (1:1—7:38) was the individual Israelite's relationship with God. God, living among His people, wanted individuals to worship Him. The person bringing an offering to God at the Tabernacle was given simple instructions for worship (1:1—6:7). Whereas the observances or feasts described in chapters 16 and 23 involved offerings for the entire nation, the sacrifices prescribed in these opening chapters were individual, private, and voluntary. Coming to worship, an individual might wish to offer praise and thanksgiving or desire to renew fellowship or seek forgiveness for sin.

No explanation of sacrifice is given; apparently the Israelites knew the significance of the sacrificial ritual. Nobody was forbidden to come to the sanctuary if he came in penitence and faith to bring an offering to the Lord, the God of Israel. Sacrifice to other gods, however, was expressly prohibited (Ex. 22:20).

Leviticus 6:8—7:36 gives instructions to the priests for officiating at the offerings brought by the laity. Very likely the first seven chapters served as a manual for the priests as they carried out their teaching responsibilities.

Moses was the person through whom God communicated these instructions (1:1; 6:8; cf. Ex. 24:16). It was Moses through whom Aaron and the priesthood were ordained to officiate at the Tabernacle (chap. 8). Moses was later recognized by Jesus as the great teacher of the law (Matt. 19:7-8; John 7:19).

With the erection of the Tabernacle, a special altar was built in the court surrounding the Tabernacle on which the Israelites were to offer sacrifices (Ex. 27:1-8, 38:1-7). That altar, called the altar of burnt offering, was the focal point where God met the Israelites. "There will I meet you and speak to you; there also will I meet with the Israelites," the Lord had assured Moses (Ex. 29:42-43). Moses officiated at that altar for the dedication of the Tabernacle and the priesthood. It was at that altar that the glory of God was manifested, confirming it as the place where the Israelites were to bring their offerings as they worshiped God. At that altar Aaron and his sons were to offer morning and evening sacrifices each day as an aroma pleasing to the Lord (Num. 28:1-8).

The burnt offering could consist of a young bull, a sheep or a goat, or a dove or a pigeon. With those options, it was possible for anyone, regardless of his resources, to offer a burnt offering. The animal, however, was to be a male "without defect," the costliest requirement in all the offerings. In this sacrifice, God required the best that man had to offer.

The procedure for bringing the offering was quite explicit.

The offerer was to bring the animal to the priest in the courtyard surrounding the Tabernacle. Before killing the animal
the offerer was to place his hand on its head, identifying it as
his substitute. After it was killed, the priest was to sprinkle its
blood on all sides of the altar. The offerer then had to skin the
animal and chop it in pieces in preparation for the sacrifice.
The entire animal except the skin, which was given to the
priest, was burned on the altar.

As the Israelite laid his hand on the animal in the presence
of the priest, he very likely offered a prayer that God would
accept his offering. As the priest applied the blood "against
the altar on all sides at the entrance to the Tent of Meeting"
(1:5), as Aaron had done in his initial burnt offering for
himself (Lev. 9:12), the offerer may have become aware of
the reality of his meeting with a holy God in worship.

The unique aspect of the burnt offering was that the entire
animal was consumed by fire on the altar. In other offerings,
a given part was withheld for the priest or for the one bringing
the offering. But the burnt offering demonstrated unreserved
consecration of the offering by the offerer.

The offerer was assured that his offering was accepted by
God as a pleasing aroma. God was pleased with the individual
Israelite who wanted to meet with Him and express his devotion by making an offering of his best, most expensive
animal. With an animal as his substitute and the applied
blood sanctifying the altar of sacrifice, the offerer could be
sure of atonement for himself, and that he as well as his offering were pleasing to God.

The word *kapar,* meaning "to atone by offering a
substitute," occurs some 49 times in Leviticus (about 150
times in the Old Testament); it usually denotes the sprinkling
of blood by the priest for the worshiper, "making an atonement" for him. The verb is usually used in connection with
the removal of sin or defilement.[2]

---

2. Gleason L. Archer, Jr., *"kapar,"* in *Theological Wordbook of the Old
Testament,* ed. R. Laird Harris, Gleason L. Archer, Jr., Bruce K. Waltke
(Chicago: Moody, 1980), 1:452-53.

Note that in the sin and guilt offerings, the main emphasis seems to be "to make atonement with them" as the priest officiates (Lev. 7:7). Specific sins are involved and confessed. Note the repeated use of the phrase "to make atonement" (4:20, 26, 31, 35; 5:6, 10, 13, 16, 18).

The morning and evening burnt offerings provided daily atonement for the sins of Israel, removing the defilement of sinful man in the presence of a holy God. The Israelites enjoyed the same relationship with God as do Christians today, who have access to daily cleansing from sin if they walk in the light (1 John 1:7-9). As God was pleased with the burnt offerings in Old Testament times, so He is pleased with offerings of praise in which Jesus Christ is acknowledged and confessed (Heb. 13:15-16).

Aaron and his sons were responsible for maintaining the daily sacrifice on the altar of burnt offering. The fire was to be kept burning throughout the night. Each morning and evening the priests had to remove the ashes and officiate at the sacrifices for the nation as well as for individuals who brought various offerings. The priests needed to be constantly vigilant; "the fire must be kept burning on the altar continuously; it must not go out" (6:13).

THE GRAIN OFFERING (2:1-16; 6:14-23)

The daily burnt offerings were immediately followed by grain offerings (cf. Num. 28:1-8). The grain offering consisted of flour and oil and did not involve animal sacrifice. A major portion was given to the priests, and a small part was burnt on the altar as "an aroma pleasing to the Lord" (2:2).

The flour and oil could be baked in an oven, prepared on a griddle, or cooked in a pan. Incense was added to the memorial portion to be burnt on the altar. The rest of the offering was considered "a most holy part" (v. 3) allotted to the priests serving at the sanctuary.

Further regulations were delineated for the priest to follow in officiating as the people brought their grain offerings to the

Tabernacle (6:14-23). When Aaron and his sons were anointed for service, they were to bring a grain offering, which was
to be consumed in its entirety on the altar; none of it was to be
eaten.

Why yeast and honey, which cause fermentation, were prohibited in the grain offering (2:11; 6:17) is not explained. Salt,
however, designated as "the salt of the covenant of your
God" (2:13), was an essential ingredient in every grain offering. In the Near East, in Old Testament times as well as today, a pact of friendship was often sealed by eating together
or by a gift of salt. Salt was also used to assure the Levites of
the tithe as their material provision: "It is an everlasting covenant of salt before the LORD for both you and your
offspring" (Num. 18:19). Salt not only provided seasoning
but also preserved the food for use by the priests as needed.
Symbolically, salt reminded the priests that God had promised part of the grain offering as a material provision for them
as they devoted their time to ministering at the Tabernacle.

This passage does not go into much detail concerning when
the grain offering was to be given, although it does state that
one occasion on which it was brought was the time of the
firstfruits, when the grain began to ripen (v. 14). Later, when
the Israelites were on the plains of Moab and Moses was giving them instructions for living in Canaan, he went into more
detail concerning this offering (Deut. 26). From the first
ripened grain, the Israelite was to bring an offering to the
priest at the Tabernacle. As the offerer acknowledged that he
was living in the land that God promised to him, the priest
would present the basket of firstfruits to the Lord at the altar.
Then the offerer was to confess that God had saved His people from Egypt and had made it possible for them to live in
Canaan. He was to conclude with the appeal, "And now I
bring the firstfruits of the soil that you, O LORD, have given
me" (Deut. 26:10). Then "before the LORD" he would bow
in worship. Together with the priests and aliens, the worshiper was to rejoice in the things God had provided for the
Israelites to enjoy.

What significance did the grain offering have for the Israelite? The burnt offering, offered daily for the nation and voluntarily by individuals, provided the offerer with the assurance that he was accepted in the presence of God at the Tabernacle. Bringing his grain offering, he worshiped in the assurance that God was pleased with his offering of the produce of his hands. It was an act of consecration and dedication to Israel's God, whom he acknowledged as his Savior.

In the fuller revelation through Jesus Christ and the New Testament, God-fearing people are frequently admonished to consecrate their lives to God (see, e.g., Rom. 12:1-2). Material blessings are to be offered back to God and shared with those who are ordained to special service (Luke 10:7; 1 Cor. 9:4-5, 13-14), even as the Israelite's offering was shared with the priests and Levites who were involved in religious service and worship.

THE FELLOWSHIP (PEACE) OFFERING (3:1-7; 7:11-38)

The fellowship offering, or peace offering, also called a sacrifice of well-being, was an optional offering in which the offerer ate part of the animal. In the burnt offering the entire animal except the skin was consumed on the altar. In the grain offering, all the grain was given to the priest except for a memorial handful, which was burned as a sacrifice. In the fellowship offering, the offerer and his family shared in a festive fellowship meal, eating the sacrificial animal near the place of sacrifice.

Cattle, sheep, and goats were used for fellowship offerings. There was no restriction to male animals as with the burnt offering. Birds, which could be offered in the burnt offering, were undoubtedly too small for the festive meal that was an essential part of the fellowship offering.

In this offering the worshiper brought his animal to the altar. Before killing the animal, the offerer laid his hand on its head and probably expressed his purpose in presenting that particular sacrifice. He perhaps wanted to praise or thank God (7:12), wanted to fulfill a particular vow, or just wanted

to express his devotion to God in a freewill offering (7:16).
Then the priest sprinkled the blood on all sides of the altar.
That reminded the offerer, as in the burnt offering, that the
blood of the substitute provided proper cleansing from defilement, which was essential in presenting an offering that
would be acceptable to a holy God. The offerer was assured
as he brought this offering that it was "an aroma pleasing to
the LORD" (3:5).

Fat was considered the choicest part of an offering (cf.
Gen. 45:18; Deut. 32:14; Ps. 81:16, "finest"). Fat around the
intestines, the kidneys, and the liver, and the fat from a
sheep's tail were burned on the altar as an offering appropriate to God alone.

In Old Testament times, kidneys and entrails were
associated with emotions in much the same way that the heart
was associated with the mind and will (cf. Jer. 4:14; 12:2).
Consequently, this offering may have symbolized the expression of the worshiper's best and deepest emotions as he
presented the choicest parts in praise and thanksgiving.[3]

The Israelites were prohibited from eating the fat and
blood of animals (7:22-27). Dietary considerations may have
been involved in the restriction against fat, although Scripture
does not say so. Since the Israelites ate butter and cheese, not
eating animal fat may have prevented an imbalance of
cholesterol as well as infestations of various parasites, such as
tapeworms, sometimes found in fatty tissue. (For the restriction against eating blood, see Leviticus 17:11.)[4]

The breast and the right leg of the animal were allotted to
the priests for their sustenance (7:28-34; 10:14-15). The rest
was given by God as a gift to the offerer.

The culmination of the ritual was a festive meal shared by
the worshiper and his family. The praise, or thank offering
(7:12-17; 22:18-30) was to be accompanied by leavened and

---

3. Gordon J. Wenham, *The Book of Leviticus* (Grand Rapids: Eerdmans,
   1979), pp. 80-81.
4. R. K. Harrison, *Leviticus* (Downers Grove, Ill.: Inter-Varsity, 1980),
   pp. 57-58.

unleavened cakes offered in thanksgiving. In a thank offering, the festive meal was restricted to the day of the sacrifice. If the offering was a freewill offering given out of devotion or an offering given in fulfillment of a vow, then the eating of the meal could continue for two days, after which any remaining meat was to be burned.

What significance did the bringing of a fellowship offering have for the Israelite worshiper? Several conclusions can be drawn from an understanding of the Hebrew word *shelem*, translated "peace," "thank," or "fellowship" offering. It refers primarily to the worshiper's experience of fulfillment, completeness, and wholeness, and above all, his personal sense of being at peace with God. Beyond the forgiveness of sin, which is assumed and basic, the individual enjoyed peace, prosperity, and the fullness of life. Out of that experience of well-being, an offering of praise and thanksgiving was a normal expression of worship. Moses repeatedly admonished the Israelites to rejoice as they came to present their offerings (Deut. 12:7, 18; 14:26).

Although the fellowship offering (3:1-17) is the third in the list of offerings (1:1—6:7), it is the last (7:11-38) in the instructions for the priests (6:8—7:38). That provides the basis for the suggestion that it was the concluding sacrifice and symbolized completeness or, possibly, the highest spiritual realization of the human-divine relationship. Could it have been the basis for Paul's assertion that Christ is "our peace" (Eph. 2:15; cf. Heb. 9:27; 10:12)?

THE SIN (PURIFICATION) OFFERING (4:1—5:13; 6:24-30)

The sin offering was introduced at Sinai, where Moses received divine revelation concerning its purpose. Before the altar of burnt offering and the Tabernacle could serve as a meeting place between God and His people, a sin offering was required. Because purification was the main element in this sacrifice, some have preferred to call it the purification offering. Sin made the people and the Tabernacle unclean. Consequently cleansing, or purification, was necessary to restore the relationship with God disrupted by uncleanness.[5]

As instructed, the Israelites had built an altar (Ex. 27:1-8; 38:1-7; 40:6-8, 29, 33), which God designated as the place where He would meet with them (Ex. 29:38-43). Vital in this relationship were the daily burnt offerings for Israel as they worshiped God.

The purpose of the sin offering was related primarily to that altar of burnt offering (Ex. 29:10-14, 36-37). In that costly sacrifice, a bull without defect, the most essential part was the blood. The fatty parts were offered on the altar, and the rest was burned outside the camp. The blood was applied to the horns of the altar, making "atonement for the altar," purging it through an act of purification so that burnt offerings could be made on it in worship of God. The original ritual of the sin offering was repeated for seven days (Lev. 8:14-17; 9:8-11, 15).

At the dedication of the Tabernacle, when the altar of burnt offering was atoned for, purified, and consecrated through the blood of the sin offering, the glory of God appeared. In a fiery divine manifestation, the offering on the altar was consumed (Lev. 9:23-24). The confirmation of God's promise that He would meet with the Israelites at that altar (Ex. 29:42-43) was witnessed by them.

Once the altar had been purified for worship, it was not required that a sin offering be offered every day, since the altar was purified daily by the blood of each burnt offering.

The sin offering was, however, required annually on the Day of Atonement (Lev. 16), when the blood from the sin offering for Aaron and his household and from the sin offering for the people was applied to the Ark of the Covenant "to make atonement for the Most Holy Place" (16:11-17). It was also applied on that day to the horns of the altar of burnt offering to make atonement for it (16:18-19). The altar of incense in all likelihood was also purified by the blood of those sin offerings (Ex. 30:7-10).

The blood of a sin offering was always applied to purify or

---

5. Wenham, pp. 88, 93-96, 146.

make holy material objects involved in a meeting between God and man. The altar of burnt sacrifice was cleansed "from the uncleanness of the Israelites" and consecrated through the application of the blood (Lev. 16:19). Atonement was made in a similar manner for "the Most Holy Place" and the Tabernacle "because of the uncleanness and rebellion of the Israelites" (Lev. 16:16). Purified through the blood of the sin offering, those objects were made "most holy, and whatever touches it will be holy" (Ex. 29:37). Consequently the offerings became holy when they were placed on the altar and thus were accepted as the Israelites offered them in worship.

When an Israelite committed unintentional sins or neglected his normal obligations, he was required to bring a sin offering. Such sins consisted in missing the mark or in not doing what was expected of him—acts of both willful disobedience and human weakness. The sin offering was compulsory for priests, the community as a whole, leaders, and the individual members of the community.

A wide variety of animals was allowed for the sin offering. Bulls, male or female goats, female lambs, doves, pigeons, and even a grain offering were acceptable. As in previous offerings, the worshiper would bring his animal to the priest, place his hand on its head while stating the reason for his offering, and then kill the animal. The priest saved the blood. Although most of the blood was poured out at the base of the altar, the priest reserved some for applying in a variety of ways, depending on the identity of the worshiper.

If an anointed priest sinned, he took the blood of a bull into the Tabernacle and sprinkled it with his finger seven times before the Lord in front of the curtain that hid the Holy of Holies, the innermost part of the Tabernacle. Then he applied some of the blood to the horns of the altar of incense (cf. Ex. 30:1-10). Returning to the altar of burnt offering, the priest would pour out the rest of the blood and offer the fatty parts of the animal on the altar. The rest of the animal was taken outside the camp, to the place where ashes were thrown, and burnt in a wood fire (4:3-12). The book of

Hebrews alludes to this procedure in speaking of Jesus' suffering outside the gate (Heb. 13:11-13).

When the offering was for the whole Israelite community, the elders brought the offering and the same ritual was followed. The priest made "atonement for them" with the assurance that "they will be forgiven" (4:13-21).

When a leader or a member of the community brought a sin offering, the priest applied the blood to the horns of the altar of burnt offering. As the worshiper and the priest completed the offering, the worshiper was assured that atonement had been made for his sin "and that he will be forgiven" (4:22-35).

Whereas Leviticus 4 describes offerings brought for unintentional sins, Leviticus 5 prescribes the sin offering for sins of omission: failure to give witness in court (v. 1), ceremonial uncleanness (vv. 2-3), and neglect of self-imposed obligations (v. 4). In each of those cases, when an individual became aware of his guilt, failure, or neglect, he was required to do something about the condition or situation that had been neglected.

If an Israelite could not afford a lamb or two doves or two young pigeons, he was allowed to substitute a tenth of an ephah (roughly two quarts or two liters) of fine flour, which represented sustenance for one full day (cf. Ex. 16:16). Although flour was a bloodless offering, the burning of a memorial portion mixed with the other burnt offerings gave it the status of a blood sacrifice. The worshiper was assured that the priest, through this offering, made atonement for him and that his sins were forgiven (5:11-13).

The sin offering of flour should not be confused with the grain offering, since it was offered without oil or frankincense. The flour replacement enforced the principle of substitution, that without the shedding of blood there is no forgiveness (Heb. 9:22).[6]

---

6. See Oswald T. Allis, "Leviticus," in *The New Bible Commentary: Revised,* ed. Donald Guthrie (Grand Rapids: Eerdmans, 1970), p. ?

When the priests were allotted a portion from the sin offering, they were to eat the meat in the courtyard of the Tabernacle (6:24-30). With great care they were to wash their blood-spattered garments and dispose of the clay pots or carefully scour the bronze pots used for cooking the meat. Any animal whose blood had been taken into the Tabernacle, however, was not to be eaten but burned (cf. 4:3-21).

The sin offering was compulsory for the Israelites who were guilty of unintentional sins and sins of contamination not committed deliberately. Repeatedly the statement occurs that when they became "aware of the sin" (4:14, 23, 28) an offering was required. When individuals were "unaware" (5:2-4) of their sin in matters of injustice, defilement, uncleanness, or thoughtlessness, a confession and a sin offering were required when they became aware of their guilt.

Cleansing, purification, sanctification, and consecration are repeatedly connected with bringing a sin offering (12:8; 14:19; 15:31). They applied to worshipers as well as to the objects used in worshiping Israel's holy God. As noted above, on the Day of Atonement the blood from the sin offering was sprinkled on various parts of the Tabernacle "to cleanse it and to consecrate it from the uncleanness of the Israelites" (16:19).

For a God-fearing Israelite, consciousness of sin necessitated atonement and forgiveness. To obtain atonement and forgiveness, he brought a sin offering for purification. For the God-fearing person since New Testament times, consciousness of sin likewise necessitates atonement and forgiveness. The apostle John describes the Christian's provision: "If we walk in the light . . . the blood of Jesus, his Son, purifies us from every sin," and, "If we confess our sins, he is faithful and just and will forgive us our sins and purify us from all unrighteousness" (1 John 1:7, 9).

THE GUILT (REPARATION) OFFERING (5:14—6:7; 7:1-7)

The guilt offering was required when an Israelite had violated the ownership rights of God or man. In addition to expiation, or atonement, complete reparation was required.

The guilt offering has often been confused with the sin offering. Consequently it is instructive to note the similarities and differences between the two offerings.

The similarities were that both:
- Were designed to reinstate the offender
- Were prescribed for specific instances of failure
- Required the burning of only the fatty parts on the altar
- Required confession
- Allotted a portion of meat to the priests
- In general, removed sin from the offender's conscience.

The guilt offering was distinct from the sin offering, however, in that:
- Expiation or atonement was made for individuals only, not for the congregation
- The offering was limited to a male ram
- Reparation or compensation was required.

The two categories of offenses for which the guilt offering was required were violations in regard to "the LORD's holy things" and property rights of man.

The sacrifice required for the guilt offering, from rich and poor alike, was a ram without defect. It was not as expensive as a bullock but much more valuable than a ewe lamb, pigeon, or dove. The priest, representing God, appraised the ram. His standard of evaluation was not the market price but "the proper value in silver, according to the sanctuary shekel" (5:15).

Trespasses in regard to any of "the LORD's holy things" involved the sanctuary and things dedicated to God. Such trespasses may have been eating the flesh of offerings or bread dedicated or set apart for the priests, or using the tithe for oneself. If someone, without knowing it, did something the Lord had prohibited and then realized his guilt (became conscience-stricken), he was required to bring a guilt offering (5:17-19).

Trespasses against a man's property rights were also "trespasses against the LORD," since they were acts of injustice against fellow men. Guilt was incurred by an individual who deceived his neighbor in matters of entrusted property (investments) or stolen property. The statement "if he cheats him" (v. 2) includes intimidating or oppressing a neighbor or taking advantage of a poor man (a translation of this verse in the Torah read "if he has intimidated his fellow."")

Finding property and denying it to the rightful owner by swearing falsely (perjury in public court) incurred guilt before the Lord that required an offering and reparation to the owner. The law specifically warned against bearing false witness (Ex. 20:16; Deut. 5:20) and defrauding a neighbor (Lev. 19:13). Love for neighbor was the admonition of Moses as well as of Paul (Lev. 19:18; cf. Rom. 13:9-10).

Reparation was the distinctive feature of the guilt offering. It required restoration of the full value plus twenty percent to the one sinned against. By offering a ram, the offender was assured of atonement and forgiveness for his wrongdoing against the Lord.

SUMMARY: OFFERINGS AND WORSHIP

As noted earlier, the worship of God was a central issue in Moses' challenge to Pharaoh to release the Israelites. Upon arrival at Mount Sinai, the Israelites accepted God's covenant with them to be His holy nation (Ex. 19-24). Most of the remaining time during that year's encampment was devoted to preparing for the worship of God, who had promised to dwell among them (Ex. 29:42-43). When the Tabernacle was dedicated and the priesthood inaugurated, the glory and presence of God was uniquely demonstrated at the altar of burnt offering in the Tabernacle courtyard (Lev. 9:23-24). God was indeed dwelling among them.

The offerings were basic to the relationship between God and Israel. Israel was God's holy people, redeemed from Egypt to worship Him exclusively. The offerings were the

---

7. *The Torah*

means by which the people were to maintain and express that exclusive relationship.

Instructions for bringing the offerings were communicated through Moses to the priests, who in turn taught the laity. Through instruction and officiating at the offerings, the priests provided the means for the Israelites to live holy lives.

The most common of the offerings, the burnt offering, was offered daily, morning and evening, on the altar of sacrifice, the appointed meeting place between God and Israel (Num. 28:1-8). As the victims were completely consumed on the altar, the burnt offerings symbolized the daily renewal of Israel's full consecration to God. Although individuals were included in the sacrifices made for the nation, any individual could bring his own burnt offering in an act of worship.

The grain offering was normally brought along with a burnt offering. In this act of dedicating the produce of his hands, the worshiper acknowledged that God was the source of material blessing. The grain offering was also a practical means of sharing with the priests what God had provided for one's livelihood. Each time the Israelite brought his grain offering in worship, he acknowledged that God was his Savior and King, who had entrusted him with the material things of daily life.

The sin offering provided purification for the Israelite so that he could approach God. This offering was required of the priest as well as of the people. As the priest entered God's presence in the Tabernacle, blood was sprinkled to purify the priests as well as the altars where the offerings were presented (Lev. 9, 16). A holy God could not dwell in surroundings defiled by uncleanness, and people and places were vulnerable to defilement and pollution by sin. The sin offering provided cleansing and sanctification so the people could come into the presence of a holy God. As individuals became conscious of sins they had committed, they could bring sin offerings and be assured of the purification they needed to make them acceptable for worshiping God.

The guilt offering primarily involved reparation of rights or property to God or man. Through this offering and proper restitution, the guilty Israelite was able to restore his relationship with God and man and be assured of the forgiveness of his sin.

The peace, or fellowship, offering was optional and voluntary. Whereas the burnt offering was essential for maintaining a continual relationship of total consecration, the grain offering acknowledged God as Savior and King, and the sin and guilt offerings were necessary for cleansing from defilement and particular sins, the fellowship offering was a voluntary expression of praise and gratitude. It was the most festive and joyous of all sacrifices. After the worshiper and the priest had shared in the offering, the worshiper and his family and friends enjoyed a festive meal in the sanctuary area.

Although atonement for sin was provided in each of the blood offerings, atonement was not their basic purpose. Israel's initial relationship with God as His redeemed people had been established through the Passover sacrifice on the night of their deliverance from Egypt. The offerings presented at the Tabernacle were the means of maintaining that relationship between the Israelites and their God.

4

CLEAN AND UNCLEAN

LEVITICUS 11:1—15:33

In the narrative of the Pentateuch, Leviticus 8-10 are followed by chapter 16. After the completion of the Tabernacle at Mount Sinai (Ex. 40) and the ordination of Aaron as high priest, the glory of God was manifested as Aaron officiated (Lev. 8-10). God, whose presence thus far had been represented in the pillar of cloud on Mount Sinai, now abode in the Tabernacle built and erected by the Israelites in the center of their encampment.

Chapter 16 records the instructions given to Aaron to make atonement for himself so that he could make atonement "for the Most Holy Place, for the Tent of Meeting and the altar, and for the priests and all the people of the community" (16:33). That ritual of atonement was to be observed once a year, on the Day of Atonement, to care for the Israelites' uncleanness (16:16, 19) so that God's presence would continue to dwell among them.

The priests were charged with the responsibility to "distinguish between the holy and the profane, between the unclean and the clean, and you must teach the Israelites all the decrees the LORD has given them through Moses" (10:10). It was a most solemn assignment. Two sons of Aaron had died suddenly for offering "unauthorized fire before the Lord" (10:1-2). Provision had already been made for a sin offering to make atonement for anyone who had become unclean (5:2-3, 5-6), and the people had been warned against bringing unclean sacrifices or offering sacrifices when they themselves were unclean (7:19-21).

For a proper understanding of the narrative of chapter 16, it is important to grasp chapters 11-15, which delineate the uncleanness of the Israelites in relation to God.

The priests were charged with teaching the Israelites concerning matters of cleanness and uncleanness in everyday life. Since the words *clean* and *unclean* occur so frequently in the book of Leviticus, and especially in chapters 11-16, the significance of those words is important, even though their precise meaning may be elusive.[1]

For the Hebrews everything was either clean or unclean, according to these instructions. Animals and foods were either clean or unclean by nature. Permanent uncleanness could not be altered but was not contagious.

Persons and objects, however, could become ritually unclean. Such uncleanness, the antithesis of holiness, was contagious. Temporary uncleanness could be incurred through childbirth, menstruation, bodily emission, "leprosy," sexual relations, misdeeds, and contact with death. Uncleanness contracted in those ways involved some degree of deviation from the usual or norm and consequently required cleansing rituals, usually over a period of time.

Clean or *cleanness* basically mean "pure," or "purity." For example, the gold covering the Ark, Mercy Seat, lampstand, and incense altar, and adorning Aaron's garments, was to be clean, or pure. Unclean persons or things could be purified by water (Lev. 11:25, 28; 14:8-9) or by fire (Num. 31:23).

The concept of cleanness seems to go beyond purity, though, in that it also connotes normality.[2] For example,

---

1. *Clean* and its derivatives occur 204 times in the Old Testament, with 44 percent in Leviticus and Numbers and 16 percent in Exodus; *unclean* and its derivatives occur 279 times in the Old Testament, with 64 percent in Leviticus and Numbers. (Edwin Yamauchi, "*taher*" and "*tame*," in *Theological Wordbook of the Old Testament,* ed. R. Laird Harris; Gleason L. Archer, Jr.; Bruce K. Waltke [Chicago: Moody, 1980], 1:343, 349.)

2. Gordon J. Wenham, *The Book of Leviticus* (Grand Rapids: Eerdmans, 1979), pp. 18-25.

when a priest pronounced a person suffering from a skin disease "clean," he undoubtedly meant the disease had taken its normal course and was no longer infectious or contagious. That person was "clean," or back to normal (13:12-17; 34-39). Sea creatures that had fins and scales, the usual aids to swimming, were clean, or normal (11:9-12). Those without the usual aids were unclean.

The converse of cleanness was uncleanness; anything or any person that was not clean was unclean. Uncleanness was incompatible with and the opposite of holiness. Cleanness, however, was not a state of holiness but "at best as a rather negative state whose existence implied that a positive holiness was attainable."[3]

Clean things had the potential of becoming holy when they were sanctified or of becoming unclean when they were polluted. In contrast to holiness, both the cleanness and the uncleanness were common. Wenham explains:

> Cleanness is the normal condition of most things and persons. Sanctification can elevate the clean into the holy, while pollution degrades the clean into the unclean. The unclean and the holy are two states which must never come in contact with each other. . . . Cleanness is the ground state; holiness and uncleanness are variations from the norm of cleanness.[4]

Consequently, the Israelites had the potential, after atonement had been made for their uncleanness, of attaining holiness through sanctification or consecration and approaching a holy God.

Holiness was a very practical problem for the Israelites because God had come to dwell among them in the Tabernacle. At the heart of the whole Sinaitic revelation, and especially in the book of Leviticus, was God's concern that the Israelites "Be holy, for I am holy" (11:44-45; 19:2;

3. R. K. Harrison, *Introduction to the Old Testament* (Grand Rapids: Eerdmans, 1969), p. 604.
4. Wenham, pp. 19-20.

20:26). Since holiness was God's essential characteristic, it was crucial that the Israelites, in their relationship with God who lived among them, be able to distinguish between the clean and the unclean. By observing the Levitical instructions, holiness was an attainable goal in everyday life as they maintained a proper reverence for God.

REGULATIONS: CLEAN AND UNCLEAN ANIMALS (11:1-47)

Leviticus 11 provides merely a listing of the various kinds of creatures that are edible, or clean, and those that are unclean and detestable. Deuteronomy 14:3-21 and other related references (Ex. 23:19; 34:26; Lev. 17:11; Deut. 12:23-25; 1 Sam. 14:32-34) supplement this list.

Following is a brief summary of this chapter's instructions.

11:1-8: Cud-chewing, cloven-hoofed animals such as the ox, sheep, and goat may be eaten. Others such as the camel, horse, and zebra are detestable.

11:9-12: Those water creatures with fins and scales are edible.

11:13-19: Clean birds may be eaten (cf. Deut. 14:11), but no identifying characteristics are listed. Most of the detestable birds listed are birds of prey that feed on carrion.

11:20-23: Flying insects that swarm may not be eaten. Those that have jointed legs for hopping, such as the locust, katydid, cricket, and grasshopper, are edible.

11:24-40: Water, vessels, and persons become unclean if they come in contact with a dead creature.

11:41-45: The summary and conclusion reiterates the simple rule, "Every creature that moves about on the ground is detestable; it is not to be eaten." The Israelites were to distinguish between the clean and the unclean because God was holy and they were to live as His holy people.

Although the distinctions between clean and unclean are explicitly delineated, the rationale for those distinctions is obscure. Since Old Testament times, numerous explanations have been offered, and we may gain some insight from discussions offered by various biblical scholars.

Gordon J. Wenham[5] lists four different kinds of explanations:
1. Arbitrary—the rationale for the rules is known only to God.
2. Cultic—animals were unclean because of use in pagan worship.
3. Hygienic—unclean creatures are unfit to eat because they are disease carriers.
4. Symbolic—the clean animals' behavior and habits that illustrate how the righteous Israelite should live; the unclean represent sinful men.

Wenham fails to find any of these explanations completely consistent and satisfactory, but he favors the views in the works of social anthropologist Mary Douglas, who advocates the interpretation that the uncleanness laws have symbolic significance.

R. K. Harrison[6] suggests the following purposes of the legislation concerning cleanness and uncleanness.
1. To avoid in Israel any resemblance to pagan religious sacrifices
2. To perpetuate Israel's separateness in dietary as well as ethical and spiritual matters
3. To provide for hygienic and dietary considerations.

He emphasizes both the importance of issues of diet, hygiene, and preventative medicine, especially in tropical and semitropical climates, and the spiritual importance that the Israelites live as God's holy people.

The division of species into clean and unclean indicates, in general, beneficial and noxious foods. It is noteworthy that the clean, edible animals were exclusively vegetarian. In a warm climate, their flesh would not decay as rapidly as that of carnivores. In the warm climate in which the Israelites lived, especially the desert, pork in particular was a source of infection.

5. Ibid., pp. 166-71.
6. Harrison, pp. 120-32.

The distinction between clean and unclean water creatures seems to be similar to that held by other ancient Near Eastern people, especially the Egyptians. By not eating crustaceans, many of which live on sewage, the Israelites may have escaped various infections and the ravages of paratyphoid fevers.

Birds that were listed as inedible or unclean, as a whole, preyed on carrion, and their flesh might transmit infection if eaten.

Locusts were commonly included in the diet of nomadic desert people. Four kinds were regarded from early antiquity as edible and were eaten in all stages of growth: the locust, the bald locust, the cricket, and the grasshopper (probably the smallest of the locust tribe). Swarming creatures or winged creeping things that move on four or more feet or crawl, including vermin and reptiles, were regarded as unclean. (Vermin and reptiles were universally regarded as unclean and not acceptable as food.)

Practical principles of hygiene may well have underlain the instructions against the contact of people or things with dead animals (11:14-40). All dead animals except those that had been ritually slaughtered were unclean. Uncleanness because of contact with dead animals was temporary, since provisions for proper cleansing were prescribed. These regulations may also reflect practical concerns about the contamination of food, water, and containers or vessels. Pollution could easily result in infection, disease, and death; consequently, preventing disease and affliction was a practical concern of everyday life.

The Israelites' dietary regulations were grounded in moral considerations. Certain fundamental principles of hygiene and diet seem to be involved and may offer limited explanations concerning some of the differentiation between the clean and the unclean; God had assured the Israelites that none of the diseases that had been divinely brought upon the Egyptians (Ex. 15:26) would come upon them if they obeyed. However, it is also reasonable to assume that these regulations were prescribed for the Israelites as measure of preventing contamination, infection, and disease.

As they observed the dietary distinctions between the clean and the unclean, the Israelites were instilled with the consciousness that they were serving the holy God dwelling among them. As God's holy people they were to remain clean so that they could be consecrated or sanctified and thus be acceptable in His presence. Uncleanness that could not be avoided in the daily responsibilities of life could be atoned for to restore one to a state of cleanness.

UNCLEANNESS FROM BODILY DISCHARGE (12:1-8; 15:1-33)

Uncleanness due to discharge through the sexual organs is discussed in chapters 12 and 15. Every person experienced such bodily discharges and was keenly aware that through them he or she became ceremonially unclean. These chapters prescribe for the removal of such uncleanness so that God's people could come into His presence in the sanctuary.

Bodily discharges that rendered a person unclean were:
1. a woman's discharge after childbirth (12:1-8)
2. a man's long-term discharge, probably due to gonorrhea (15:2-3). (Although it is not explicitly stated that the discharge in 15:2-3 is genital, it seems to be a reasonable inference. The Septuagint translation recognizes it as gonorrhea.)[7]
3. a man's emission of semen (15:16-18)
4. a female's discharge in her menstrual period (15:19-24)
5. a female's long-term discharge (15:25-27).

Uncleanness because of human discharge could defile others. It was more contagious or infectious than the uncleanness from unclean animals or skin diseases. It was also transmitted to objects such as chairs and beds that were touched by an unclean person (15:4-12, 17, 26-27). Spittle from an unclean person also was infectious, and clay pots (cooking vessels) he touched had to be destroyed (v. 12; cf. 11:32-33). Anyone who came in direct contact with a person

---

7. Wenham, pp. 217-18.

who was unclean because of any of the five reasons listed above, or with any objects used by such a person, became unclean.

In New Testament times a woman who had been suffering from a discharge of blood for twelve years was fearful of confessing that she had touched Jesus (Mark 5:25-34). Under Levitical law she would have contaminated Jesus and made Him unclean. However, Jesus did not ostracize her but healed her.

All of the people affected by the uncleanness described in these chapters could remove their uncleanness by washing with fresh water. Washing also restored unclean objects (with the exception of clay pots) to a clean state. After purification with water, unclean persons and objects were declared clean by the end of the day.

Three of the five sources of uncleanness, men's or women's long-term bodily discharge and childbirth, required offerings at the Tabernacle after the restoration of cleanness through water purification. In each of those, uncleanness lasted more than seven days.

For both men and women with long-term discharge, the requirements were the same (15:13-15, 28-30). After the discharge had ceased, they were to wait seven days, bathe themselves, and wash their clothes in order to be restored to a state of cleanness. On the eighth day they were to bring an offering of two young pigeons or doves to the priest at the Tabernacle. One bird was presented as a sin, or purification, offering, with the priest applying the blood to the altar to purify it and the Tabernacle (Lev. 4:3-7). The other was presented as a burnt offering, expressing gratitude and renewed dedication to God and assuring the offerer of forgiveness of sin. Through those offerings atonement was made for the uncleanness of bodily discharge (15:15, 30).

That appearance at the Tabernacle must have been a very meaningful experience of acknowledging God's goodness in restoration. Whether the time of bodily discharge had been brief or extended, it had barred the victim from worship at the Tabernacle. Had he or she gone to the Tabernacle while unclean, he or she would have polluted the Tabernacle and would have been liable to death under divine judgment. These offerings restored the privilege of worshiping God, expressing thankfulness, and rejoicing in the presence of God.

An offering was required for a mother after childbirth. Her uncleanness was not due to childbirth but to the resultant flow of blood (12:4, 5, 7) similar to her menstrual period. A mother was unclean for seven days after the birth of a son and fourteen days after the birth of a daughter. During that time she was contagious, making people and objects she touched unclean. During her time of purification—thirty-three days after the birth of a son and sixty-six days after the birth of a daughter—she was not contagious, but she was still not permitted to worship at the Tabernacle. Unfortunately for our inquisitive minds, Scripture does not explain the different lengths of the period of purification after the birth of a son and a daughter.

The Israelites were to acknowledge the birth of a child as a gift of God resulting from the normal sexual functions God had provided. Even at birth, parents were conscious that man was subject to sin and death, as pronounced to Adam and Eve and experienced by subsequent generations. As David confessed after his sexual immorality, human beings are tainted with sin from conception (Ps. 51:5). During an extended time after the birth of each child, as parents reflected on man's limitations, they had the assurance that their uncleanness would pass and they could return to the Tabernacle and be accepted in the presence of their holy God.

Their return to the Tabernacle must have been a most gratifying experience. For the burnt offering they were required to bring a year-old lamb, as in the initial Passover in Egypt (Ex. 12:5; 29:38), or a substitute if they could not afford a lamb. A sin offering cleansed the altar and sanctuary (4:3-6), and the burnt offering provided assurance of the forgiveness of sin, for which they were grateful to God. This special occasion was a time of rejoicing and giving of thanks to God for His gift of a child.

After her purification, the mother was required to bring offerings so that the priest could "make atonement for her, and then she will be ceremonially clean from her flow of blood" (12:7). For her sin offering she was to bring a young pigeon or dove, and for her burnt offering a year-old lamb. If she could not afford a lamb, she could substitute a dove or a pigeon. Through those offerings the priest made atonement for her and she was declared clean (12:8).

The source of uncleanness described in these chapters is human discharge through the sexual organs. None of these discharges was pronounced sinful in itself, but each was declared unclean and disqualified one from coming into the presence of God.

God created man and woman with sexual differences and gave them the mandate to bear children (Gen. 1:28; cf. 9:1). God's promise was vested in the seed of the woman (Gen. 3:15). Consequently childbirth was a normal expectation. Yet intercourse caused the most serious and prolonged uncleanness apart from uncured skin diseases (Lev. 13-14).

In the Near East of Moses' day, especially in Canaan, prostitutes were attached to religious shrines and sanctuaries. Serving the deities of those religious centers usually included sexual activity. In pagan religions, a man's most important act might be his copulation with a dedicated prostitute in the hope that the deities would provide him with fertile plants and animals.

Through the Levitical regulations, God's people were impressed with the fact that sexual activity, though not in itself sinful, had no place at the Tabernacle, especially not in the abusive form the pagan Canaanites gave it. Prostitution and child sacrifice had no place in God's holy sanctuary. The Israelites should have been repulsed by the abuse of sex as they contemplated association or intermarriage with the Canaanites (Ex. 34:15-16; Lev. 18).

Israel did not have male and female deities as did their pagan neighbors. The God of Israel was not a sexual Being. Jesus taught that after death, men and women will not be involved in the sexual relationship of marriage (Matt. 22:30; Mark 12:25). Sexuality and marriage, which cease with death, were to be used properly by the Israelites in relationship with their holy God.

In the days of Eli, when the Israelites had lived in Canaan for centuries, the significance of the relationship of sex and the sensual to the Tabernacle is vividly demonstrated. On the one hand, the priest's sons Hophni and Phinehas, guilty of sexual immorality (1 Sam. 2:22), were divinely judged. On the other hand, Hannah came with a more expensive offering than was required and expressed her thanksgiving and gratitude to God for the gift of a son (1 Sam. 1:24—2:10).

The sudden death of Eli and his sons allowed the Ark of God to fall into Philistine hands and the Tabernacle to be destroyed, and "the glory" of the Lord's presence in the Tabernacle departed from Israel (1 Sam. 4:21-22). However, God's future blessings were not bound to the Tabernacle or to the official priesthood, as shown by the life of the son born to a praying mother who had dedicated him to God.

The banning of the sexual and the sensual from the presence of God (Ex. 19:15, 20:26; Lev. 15:16-18) may have been one of the most noteworthy characteristics of Israel's religion, uniquely distinguishing it from the other religions of the ancient Near East.

UNCLEANNESS FROM SERIOUS SKIN DISEASES (13:1—14:57)

In Israel, uncleanness could also be caused by infectious skin diseases. Instructions for diagnosing and removing uncleanness are detailed in chapters 13 and 14.

The skin diseases under consideration in these chapters are identified by the Hebrew word *sara at,* an exhibit of a swelling, eruption, or an inflamed spot on the surface of one's body (13:2-46; 14:1-32). The same word is used for a degenerative growth such as mold or mildew in woolen or linen garments (13:47-58), for mineral eruptions on walls, and for what may have been dry rot in the structure of buildings (14:33-53). The word is generic rather than specific, describing a broad range of ailments.

The Greek translation of this word in the Septuagint is *lepra,* by which medical authors described a cutaneous eruption that made the skin flaky or scaly and was possibly similar to the leprosy known since 1871 as Hansen's disease. The Latin translation in the Vulgate adopted *lepra* to designate leprosy.

Sara at apparently included a broad class of ailments, only one of which was Hansen's disease. R. K. Harrison "prefers to use the term 'leprosy' for *sara at,* regarding it as a general designation of a class of skin afflictions of varying severity." He believes that clinical leprosy, familiar in the ancient Near East since around 2000 B.C., very likely was known to the Israelites in Egypt.[8]

These skin diseases were identified by eruptions similar to those that could affect houses, through mineral efflorescence (14:44); leather (13:56); and clothing (13:37, 59). Tissue inflammation or abnormal cutaneous conditions aroused suspicions of leprosy. After a period of quarantine, malignancy could be detected. However these passages do not describe leprosy but such skin diseases as psoriasis, favus, leucodemia (vitilego), acne, alopecia, and other conditions known to modern physicians.

These chapters identify these skin diseases and give instructions and general principles to guide the priest in examining the sufferer. These instructions and regulations were given to them through Moses and Aaron (13:1; 14:1, 33). The language of the Hebrew text is similar to that of Eygptian medical texts. Consequently if the modern reader finds these chapters somewhat obscure, he should recall that they are written in the technical language of textbooks.

---

8. R. K. Harrison, *Leviticus* (Downers Grove, Ill.: Inter-Varsity, 1980), pp. 136-39; *Introduction to the Old Testament,* pp. 607-10.

The priest's responsibility was to examine a person's symptoms and then distinguish between a clean and an unclean condition; he was not a physician who diagnosed what a particular disease might be or determined its underlying cause.

The following conditions merited examination:

1. A swelling or shiny rash (13:2-8). If the hair in the rash had turned white, the person was unclean. (This may have been psoriasis.) If not, judgment was suspended for seven days of testing.

2. Raw flesh with white hair (13:9-17). However if this covered the entire body, possibly causing the skin to peel as in dermatitis or scarlet fever, a quarantine was not necessary, and the man was declared clean.

3. A boil on the skin resulting in inflammation (13:18-28). White hair and reddish-white spots made a person unclean. (This may have been identified palsy, eczema, or favus.) Another examination was conducted after seven days.

4. A sore on the head or chin (13:29-37). The priest was to determine whether or not it was infected below the skin. If it did not appear so, a seven-day period of isolation was required before the priest could pronounce cleanness or uncleanness. Because the yellowing of hair was a criterion in the diagnosis, it has been suggested that this disease was favus.

5. White spots on the skin (vv. 38-39). If the spots were dull white, the person was declared clean. This may have been vitilego or leucorderma.

6. Reddish-white sores on a bald spot (vv. 40-44). This may have been psoriasis. (Baldness or partial baldness, however, did not render a person unclean.)

A person declared by the priest to have an infectious skin disease that might defile others was required to demonstrate his uncleanness publicly. With torn clothes, untidy hair, and a covering over the lower part of his face, the diseased person was to cry, "Unclean," warning those around him not to defile themselves by contact with him. As long as his infectious disease remained, he was to live outside the camp.

Such uncleanness not only made him a social outcast but barred him from the Tabernacle. Living outside the covenant community, he was not covered by the morning and evening sacrifices for the congregation of Israel. Neither could he come to the Tabernacle to offer sacrifices for himself.

Infectious skin diseases (*sara at*) in linen, wool, or leather clothing were also subject to examination by the priest (13:47-59). Mold or mildew would disfigure clothing just as a cutaneous infection would disfigure a person. Both might cause peeling or flaking. If the priest diagnosed mildew spreading in a knitted or woven garment or leather article after a seven-day quarantine, then the mildew was declared destructive and the garment or article was burned. Even if the mildew did not spread, the clothing or article was to be washed and isolated for another seven days. If the appearance of the mildew had not changed, even though it had not spread, the garment had to be burned. If the mildew had become pale, then the garment could be kept if the part that had been affected by the mildew were removed. After a second washing, such a garment could be declared clean. However, should mildew break out again, the garment had to be destroyed.

Unclean garments and articles had to be destroyed by fire. Unclean persons who were not cured were isolated from the camp of Israel and denied access to the Tabernacle where God had chosen to dwell.

But a person so ostracized from God's people and a house that had been affected by an infectious skin disease could be restored. Chapter 14 describes the cleansing process.

The priest had responsibility for supervising the diagnosis and the cleansing ritual after a person had been cured. Unlike the pagan priests of surrounding nations, whose exorcism and magical rites involved dubious attempts at healing the afflicted, the Israelite priest did not offer healing. No cure for infectious skin diseases is prescribed in these instructions. For that the Israelite was directly dependent upon God.

When a person recovered from his disease, the priest was summoned outside the camp to examine him (14:2-9). If the priest was satisfied that he was cured, that person was to have two birds brought (most likely by friends) for the ritual of restoration to the camp. The procedure in this ritual is significant. One bird was killed and its blood drained into a clay pot of fresh water. The other bird was dipped in that water-blood mixture. After the live bird had been dipped, it was held while the priest dipped cedar wood, scarlet yarn and hyssop into the same mixture and sprinkled the restored person seven times. Then the man was pronounced clean, and the live bird was released into the open fields.

After that, the person washed his clothes, shaved off all his hair, and bathed in water, which made him ceremonially clean so that he could return to the camp. He was restricted from entering his tent, however, for seven days. On the seventh day he repeated the washing and shaving and was again declared clean, restored to the privilege of worship at the Tabernacle.

The ceremony with birds is without parallel or interpretation in Scripture. Although one bird was killed, nothing is said about offering it as a sacrifice. Furthermore, the ritual took place outside the camp, not at an altar or the Tabernacle.

The focus of this unique rite was the blood that was applied to the other bird and to the cured person. No doubt that application of blood brought home to him the fact that a life had been given so that he could be released from his exile from the camp.

At the confirmation of the covenant at Mount Sinai, Moses had sprinkled blood on the altar and on the people as a symbol of their special relationship with God (Ex. 24:6-8). Here outside the camp there apparently was no altar or sacrifice. Thus it was the sprinkled blood that assured the cured man that he was clean and acceptable before God as one of the covenant congregation.

When the cured person heard the priest publicly pronounce

him clean and saw the bird fly away, new hope dawned. Instead of returning to isolation, he could now go with his friends to shave, bathe, and clothe himself, and reenter the camp and return to his home. Furthermore, he could look forward to going to the Tabernacle to present his offerings and worship. For his offerings he was instructed to bring two male lambs, one ewe, flour for grain offering, and one log of oil. With the priest officiating, he was to offer a guilt (reparation) offering (cf. Lev. 5), a sin (purification) offering (cf. Lev. 4), and a burnt offering (cf. Lev. 11), together with a grain offering (cf. Lev. 2). The peace, or fellowship, offering, which was usually voluntary, was not required.

It is interesting that he was to begin his worship with a guilt offering, which was usually prescribed for those who had committed "a violation and sins unintentionally in regard to any of the LORD's holy things" (5:14). However, no restitution payment was required with this offering (14:10; cf. 5:14-19). The priest applied the blood of the guilt offering to the right ear, thumb, and toe of the offerer (14:14) as had been done at the ordination of Aaron and his sons (8:24). Then the priest sprinkled the oil before the Lord seven times, applied the oil to the person's right ear, thumb, and toe, and poured the remaining oil on his head. Since this was a special ritual not normally prescribed for a guilt offering (see 6:14-19; 7:1-10), the cured person must have been doubly assured that "atonement for him before the LORD" was made (14:18). Just as the Tabernacle, all that was in it, and the priests were consecrated and ready for worship, so now he was consecrated and ready to bring his offerings before God.

Scripture does not tell us why this cured person was required to bring a guilt offering as he came to worship. Although individuals were sometimes afflicted with serious skin diseases as punishment for sacrilegious behavior (cf. Num. 12:9; 2 Kings 5:27; 2 Chron. 26:17), nothing in this text indicates that such diseases were always a result of sin (cf. John 9:1-3). Very likely this guilt offering was to make him aware that during his time of uncleanness he had not brought his sacrifices, tithes, and firstfruits to God, even though his neglect had been beyond his control.

After the guilt offering, the cured man brought his sin (purification) offering. In this offering, the blood played the most important part, providing cleansing for the sanctuary and the altar (Ex. 29:10-14, 36-37). Next came the burnt offering, through which the person was reconciled to God and dedicated his life to the service of God. With the grain offering he made his pledge of allegiance.

If he was very poor, the cured man could substitute two doves or two pigeons for the lamb and ewe required for the guilt and burnt offerings (vv. 21-31). But for the guilt offering no substitution was allowed; a lamb was required.

With those ceremonies, a person who had been ostracized from the camp of Israel because of infectious skin disease could be restored to life in the covenant community. Now he was included in the offerings made daily for Israel, and he could personally bring his offerings and worship at the Tabernacle.

5

THE DAY OF ATONEMENT

The Day of Atonement was the most solemn day of the Israelites' religious year. Instructions for its observance were given immediately following the dedication of the Tabernacle and the death of Nadab and Abihu (chaps. 8-10). Thus chapter 16 continues the narrative that focuses on the Tabernacle as the meeting place between God and Israel (cf. Ex. 40; Lev. 8-10).

The basic purpose of the ceremonies and offerings of the Day of Atonement was to make atonement for Israel's sin (vv. 16, 21, 30). It was crucial that the Israelites, who were constantly vulnerable to sin and uncleanness (see chaps. 11-15), have a way to be restored to fellowship with the holy God dwelling among them. On the Day of Atonement, uncleanness was removed from the worshipers and the Tabernacle so that God could be worshiped in purity and holiness.

As he officiated on this solemn occasion, Aaron was to wear simple garments (vv. 3-4), plainer than the attire of ordinary priests (Ex. 39:27-39). No reason is given for this simple attire, a contrast to the splended clothes he usually wore (see Ex. 28), but it has been suggested that elaborate garments might have detracted from the somberness of the occasion, when atonement for sin was the basic concern.

For the offerings on this day, one young bullock, two rams and two goats were brought to the entrance of the Tabernacle. Aaron cast lots to decide which of the two goats should be sacrificed as a sin offering for the people.

With the blood from the bull killed for his own sin offer-

ing, a censer full of burning coals from the main altar, and
two handfuls of incense, Aaron entered the Tabernacle. The
incense was placed on the coals, creating smoke to conceal the
atonement cover of the Ark as Aaron approached it to
sprinkle the bull's blood once on its front and seven times
before it (vv. 11-14). Aaron then killed the goat that had been
chosen as an offering on behalf of the Israelites and did the
same with its blood. In that manner atonement was made
"for the Most Holy Place because of the uncleanness and
rebellion of the Israelites, whatever their sins have been" and
for the Tabernacle located in the midst of their uncleanness
(v. 16).

Returning to the altar of sacrifice, Aaron took blood from
both the goat and the bull and sprinkled the altar seven times
to "cleanse and to consecrate it from the uncleanness of the
Israelites" (vv. 18-19).

On the Day of Atonement, Aaron was the sole represen-
tative for his family and the entire congregation of Israel. No
one else was allowed in the Tabernacle on that solemn occasion. Through applying the blood of the sin offerings, Aaron
"made atonement for himself, his household and the whole
community of Israel" (v. 17), and for the Most Holy Place,
the Tabernacle, and the altar (v. 20).

Returning to the altar, Aaron directed his attention to the
live goat. Laying both hands on its head he publicly confessed
"all the wickedness and rebellion of the Israelites—all their
sins—and put them on the goat's head" (v. 21). Then a man
appointed for the task took the goat out to the solitude of the
desert and abandoned him. Before returning to the camp,
that man was required to bathe and clothe himself anew.

The sin offering of two goats was unique to the Day of
Atonement. The blood of one provided cleansing so the people could approach God. The other was "for Azazel" (vv. 8,
10, 26), or a scapegoat.[1]

---

1. For a discussion of numerous interpretations, see Gordon J. Wenham,
Leviticus (Grand Rapids: Eerdmans, 1979), pp. 233-35.

The symbolism is clear. Sin was removed from the camp of Israel, where God had His abode among them, to the place of uncleanness. Sin was exterminated from the camp of Israel and the presence of God.

Having made atonement through the sin offering, Aaron returned to the Tabernacle to remove his linen garments, bathe himself, and dress in his regular garments. Then, returning to the altar, he offered two rams as a burnt offering and burned the fat of the sin offering, making atonement for himself and the Israelites (vv. 23-25).

The carcasses of the bull and the goat, which had provided the blood for the sin offerings, were then taken outside the camp, where they were burned up, hide, flesh, and dung. They were totally consumed, except for their blood, which had been used to make atonement for sin. The man who burned those animals was also required to bathe and change clothes before returning to the camp (vv. 27-28).

The members of the congregation were to assemble before the Tabernacle once a year to take part in this solemn meeting with the God who was dwelling among them to be cleansed from sin (vv. 29-33). The people were to deny and afflict themselves on this day (vv. 29-33; 23:27, 32; Num. 29:7), very likely by fasting, mourning, and confessing sin (cf. the context of Ps. 35:13 and Isa. 58:3, 5, where the same words, "deny" and "afflict," are used.)

Conscious of their need for cleansing from sin in order to approach a holy God, the Israelites were assured that the blood of the sin offering removed their uncleanness and the uncleanness of all the material things used in their approach to God—the Tabernacle, the altar, and the Ark of the Covenant with its cover of the Mercy Seat. The priest who represented them was also cleansed. Thus the removal of sin was vividly portrayed.

In the New Testament, Paul, reflecting on man's need for cleansing from sin, uses several expressions in his letter to the Romans that reflect the uniqueness of the sin offering of the Day of Atonement. He asserts that God sent "his own son in

the likeness of sinful man to be a sin offering" (8:3) and that
Christ "was delivered over to death for our sin" (4:25). To
the Corinthians he pointed out that God made Jesus "who
had no sin to be sin for us" (2 Cor. 5:21), perhaps an allusion
to the Day of Atonement ritual of the sins of Israel being laid
symbolically on the live goat. Bearing Israel's sin, that goat
was delivered over to death in the wilderness. Jesus also died
to remove man's sin.

The blood of Christ provided access to God, even as the
blood sprinkled by the priest provided access to God in the
Tabernacle. Paul asserts that God has presented Jesus "as a
sacrifice of atonement, through faith in his blood" (Rom.
3:25). It is through Christ that "we have gained access" to
and have peace with God (Rom. 5:12). The removal of sin is
basic to access to God.

The author of the book of Hebrews, writing to Christians
who were more familiar with the Old Testament, uses the Day
of Atonement ritual as the basis for his description of the
God-man relationship established through Jesus Christ, com-
paring Christ's entrance to heaven with the "every year" entrance of the high priest (9:25). In emphasizing our free access
to God through the blood of Christ, he reminded his readers
that the high priest entered "only once a year, and never
without blood" (9:7). Christ thus entered the Most Holy
Place by merit of His own blood and thus did away with the
need to repeat that ritual annually (10:1-10).

Although he does not refer directly to the scapegoat that
was abandoned to death, the writer of Hebrews does assert
that Christ "died as a ransom to set them free from the sins
committed under the first covenant" (9:15). In the sin offering of the Day of Atonement, both the live goat and the body
of the goat that provided the blood for atonement were
removed outside the camp, the former relegated to death and
the latter to a consuming fire. The comment that "Jesus also
suffered outside the city gate" (13:12) brings into focus the
fact that Christ was crucified outside the city of Jerusalem, in
which the Temple was located.

What happened on the day the blood of Jesus was shed outside the gate is recorded in three accounts (Matt. 27:51; Mark 15:38; Luke 23:45): the veil in the Temple was torn in two, providing access to the Most Holy Place. Peter asserts that Jesus "bore our sins in his body on the tree" (1 Pet. 2:24). While sin was being removed through Christ's bearing man's sin in His body outside the city, the Most Holy Place was unveiled in Jerusalem, making access to God, previously reserved for the high priest, possible for all.

The author of Hebrews emphasizes that this access to God was provided through Christ as He "entered the Most Holy Place once for all by his own blood, having obtained eternal redemption" (9:12). Thus Jesus Christ provided both the removal of sin and the access to God that were annually portrayed to the Israelites on the Day of Atonement.

For those who accept Jesus Christ as the fulfillment of the foreshadowing of the Day of Atonement sacrifice, the annual remembrance of Christ's crucifixion is very significant. The author of Hebrews admonishes us "to enter the Most Holy Place by the blood of Jesus, by a new and living way opened for us through the curtain, that is, his body" (10:19-20). With sin removed and access to God provided through Jesus Christ, we can freely draw near to God through faith.

The sin offering did not initiate a relationship with God but was essential to maintaining or restoring that relationship by cleansing Israel from unintentional sins and the sins of omission (cf. Lev. 4:1—5:13; 6:24-30). The author of Hebrews indicates that that blood was applied in the Most Holy Place "for the sins the people had committed in ignorance" (9:7). Thus the Israelites never gained perfection in this life but were reminded annually that they needed cleansing. At the same time, the sin offering on the Day of Atonement made it possible for God to continue to dwell among His people and have a relationship with them.

Having access to God through Christ, who opened the way for us, we can come continually into God's presence. The apostle John writes, "If we walk in the light . . . the blood of Jesus, his Son, purifies us from every sin. . . . If we confess our sins, he . . . will forgive us our sins and purify us from all unrighteousness" (1 John 1:7-9). Like the Israelites, we have a divine provision for cleansing from the sins that are common to us as we live in this world, and we can have God's presence abiding with us in our daily lives.

6

LIVING AS GOD'S HOLY PEOPLE

LEVITICUS 17:1—22:33

The first sixteen chapters of Leviticus are concerned primarily with establishment and maintainance of the relationship between Israel and God. That God should have a dwelling place in the camp of Israel was a unique situation. Other nations had temples for manmade gods. By contrast, the Israelites had a living, active God, who had delivered them from Egyptian bondage and now was dwelling among them, His chosen people.

When the Tabernacle was completed and sanctified (made holy) through the blood of the sin offering, God's presence was vividly manifested (8:10). Through the offerings, that relationship could be maintained (chaps. 1-7). Cleansing from the uncleanness incurred in the course of everyday life (chaps. 11-15) was provided annually on the Day of Atonement (chap. 16). In those ways, the human-divine relationship was continually maintained so that the Israelites could worship God.

ETHICAL HOLINESS IN EATING (17:1-16)

In chapter 17, the emphasis shifts to the affairs of the everyday life of the Israelites as God's holy people. Conscious of God's presence among them, how were they to live? Negatively, they were warned against conforming to the immoral and idolatrous practices of the Egyptians and Canaanites in whose cultures they lived. Consequently, laws and principles were designed to keep them from involvement in pagan practices.

Chapter 17 gives instructions concerning the killing of animals and the eating of blood. For the Israelites during their wilderness journey, killing domestic animals was restricted to the Tabernacle, under the supervision of the priests. The Tabernacle was in the middle of the camp of Israel, and the people were prohibited from making sacrifices in open fields or offering them to goat idols or goat demons in the wilderness (vv. 1-9). The first commandment, basic to all the others, was exclusive devotion to God. The worship of other gods, especially demons, was to be avoided through the commandment to kill all animals at the Tabernacle. The Israelites had already been warned about participating in idolatrous worship that involved prostitution (Ex. 34:15-16).

The second prohibition was the eating of blood (vv. 10-12). With animal slaughter limited to the Tabernacle and the priest applying the blood to the altar to make it holy, the Israelites were repeatedly reminded that it was through blood that atonement was made. Blood was the price paid for their ransom.

The blood of wild animals, which naturally could not be brought to the Tabernacle for slaughter, was to be drained and covered with earth (vv. 13-14). If anyone ate meat from which the blood had not been drained properly, ceremonial cleansing was required in order to restore him to a state of cleanness (vv. 15-16).

To eat blood was also to misuse that which was at the heart of the Israelites' relationship with God. It was the blood of an animal that provided the way for man to appear in the presence of God. Consequently, it was a serious offense to disobey the prohibition against eating blood. Eating blood indicated a lack of respect for life.

The consequences of disobedience were severe. An individual who disregarded these prohibitions was subject to being "cut off from his people" (vv. 4, 10, 14). Such offenses were considered as serious as murder and merited divine punishment.

Whether the expression "cut off" means premature death

or judgment in the life to come is not clearly indicated in this text. That the consequence was of a most serious and awesome nature may be supported by the additional clause, "I will set my face against that person" (v. 10). Any violation of these two basic prohibitions was a matter of ultimate consequence. But in obeying them, the Israelites were able to live as God's holy people.

The commandment to kill animals only at the Tabernacle was temporary, applying to the Israelites' encampment in the wilderness. Before Moses died, he told the people that after they had settled in Canaan, it would not be necessary to bring their animals to the central sanctuary for slaughter. They could then slaughter their animals and eat meat in any of their towns (Deut. 12:15, 20-21). The prohibition against eating blood, however, remained.

The context in which Moses gave these instructions indicates a basic problem concerning the slaughter of animals. In Canaan, the Israelites were to "destroy all the places . . . where the nations you are dispossessing worship their gods" (Deut. 12:2). Moses warned them, "You must not worship the LORD your God in their way" (12:4). If they obeyed those commands, then the slaughter of animals for food would not be associated with heathen practices.

Thus it was in the context of a pagan culture that the Israelites were instructed to live as God's holy people, exclusively devoted to God. They were to be very careful that not even in the slaughter of animals would they take up the pagan practices associated with worshiping other gods or demons.

The New Testament tells how the early Christians, at the Jerusalem Council, dealt with the basic problem of acknowledging idols. Gentiles who turned to God were warned to abstain from food sacrificed to idols and from meat of strangled animals and from blood (Acts 15:20, 29). Paul acknowledged that the meat of the slaughtered animal was not itself affected when offered to idols (Rom. 14:2-3, 14-18; 1 Cor. 8:1-13; 10:25—11:1). At issue, as it had been for ancient Israel, was the acknowledgement or recognition of idols. Both Paul and Moses insisted on exclusive devotion to God. For the Israelites, in their unique experience of God dwelling among them, it was important that the slaughter of animals be limited to the Tabernacle lest they give the appearance of recognizing the idols of the people about them. There was no compromise for the Israelites in the matter of worship. When they transgressed and sacrificed to demons, they were severely judged (Num. 25; Deut. 32:17). Jesus, before He died, taught that His shed blood was essential for making atonement, reaffirming the ancient identification of life with blood. As the author of Hebrews explains, "Without the shedding of blood there is no forgiveness" (9:22). Speaking of the wine, the symbol of His blood soon to be shed, Jesus told His disciples, "This is the blood of the covenant, which is poured out for many for the forgiveness of sins" (Matt. 26:28). Thus for Christians it is not abstinence from eating blood but the repeated remembrance of the shed blood of Christ that conveys the message of the forgiveness of sin.

ETHICAL HOLINESS IN CHASTITY (18:1-30)

Sexual perversion seems to have been a besetting sin since the beginning of the human race. The sexual practices listed in chapter 18 may have been common to the Egyptians and the Canaanites (v. 3). God, who created man, deems these practices so abominable that He specifically designated them to be abhorred by the Israelites.

Six times in this passage God identifies Himself, "I am the LORD (your God)" (vv. 2, 4, 5, 6, 21, 30). That should have reminded them that it was God who had delivered them out of Egyptian slavery (Ex. 20:22). They owed their freedom and existence as a nation to God; they had been chosen to be God's holy nation (Ex. 19:4-6).

Seven times the Israelites were reminded not to conform to the sexual practices of the nations about them (vv. 3, 24, 26-30). They were not to be influenced by nor imitate the sexual immorality of the Egyptians or the Canaanites. Through child sacrifice (v. 21), sexual perversion (vv. 22-24), and other detestable practices, the surrounding nations had defiled themselves, incurring divine judgment. The Israelites were warned that those who participate in such practices would be cut off from their people.

Although some of the same incestuous relationships were forbidden in the Code of Hammurabi and the Hittite laws, the longer list of forbidden unions (vv. 6-18) distinguished Israel from culture contemporary to her. Homosexuality, bestiality, and other perversions common to the Canaanites, Egyptians, Hittites, and Phoenicians were forbidden to Israel (vv. 19-23).

The Israelites were warned not to "profane the name of your God" (v. 21). Using God's name in vain (19:12), idol worship (Ezek. 20:39), and disregard for the Sabbath were all forms of profanation, which would make the Tabernacle (21:12, 23) and sacred offerings (22:15) unholy. As God's holy people they were to reflect the holiness of God.

Misuse of the body, especially in sexual abuses, was abhorrant to God. Five times in this chapter (vv. 22, 26-30), deviant sexual practices are called "detestable," and the Israelites were warned to abhor them.

The Israelites were expected to observe these prohibitions because they belonged to the God who reminded them, "I am the LORD" (v. 5). Living by these laws would not make them God's people; rather, obedience was to be the result of their having become God's people. Likewise the New Testament prohibits incest (1 Cor. 5:1-2), adultery (Rom. 13:9), idolatry (Rev. 2:14), and homosexuality (Rom. 1:27; 1 Cor. 6:9) for those who are God's people today.

GOD-CONSCIOUSNESS IN EVERYDAY LIFE (19:1-37)

The Israelites were expected as a community to reflect God's holiness. Whereas the previous chapters prohibited individual sexual perversion, the emphasis in chapter 19 is primarily on their everyday relationships with their neighbors, in which they were expected to demonstrate a consciousness of God's presence.

This chapter contains twenty-eight negatives. Most prohibit actions toward fellow men that are contrary to God's attitude toward them. Even the Ten Commandments, which are included here, contain eleven prohibitions. In their cultural context, it was essential that the Israelites realize that as God's holy people they needed to be distinctive, not conforming to the patterns of the nations around them.

Basic to these negatives is the positive relationship between God and Israel. The statement "I am the LORD (your God)" concludes each of sixteen paragraphs dealing with the affairs of human life (vv. 3-36). The opening words of the chapter highlight the God-man relationship: "Be holy, because I the LORD your God, am holy" (v. 2*b*), and the chapter closes with the reminder "Keep all my decrees and all my laws and follow them. I am the LORD" (v. 37).

The underlying emphasis of this chapter is maintaining a daily relationship with God:

•do not turn to idols or make gods (v. 4)
•bring offerings as prescribed (vv. 5-8)
•do not profane the name of God (v. 12)
•revere God (v. 14; cf. v. 32)
•keep my decrees (v. 19; cf. also v. 37)
•do not practice divination or sorcery (v. 27).

Reverence for a holy God was to be expressed in honoring parents (cf. Ex. 20:13) as representatives of God and in worshiping God by observing the Sabbath (v. 3). Obedience to those statutes was basic to the Israelites' position as God's holy people. Having been redeemed, they were never to forget that God had chosen them to live holy lives. They were to be conscious of the presence of a holy God and were not to allow any behavior, whether through negligence or deliberate intention, to mar their relationship with God.

That vertical relationship was to be reflected horizontally with their neighbors (vv. 9-18). In harvesting they should be generous, allowing the poor and needy to gather the gleanings, reflecting in a practical way God's concern for the poor. Stealing, lying, deception, swearing falsely, defrauding, robbing, withholding wages, taking advantage of the handicapped, perverting justice, slander, endangering life, bearing a grudge, hatred—all were offenses against neighbors. Given human nature, they most likely were common offenses. That list of prohibitions should have impressed on the Israelites that they were not to conform behaviorally to the peoples about them but reflect God's holy character in their community.

The positive aspect of those prohibitions is expressed in the short, concise phrase "Love your neighbor as yourself" (v. 18). It was the moral concept that uniquely distinguished the Israelites in the ancient world. (Jesus also emphasized it as basic and, together with love for God, as the essence of the entire Old Testament revelation [Matt. 19:19; 22:39; Mark 12:31; Luke 10:27].) With this in mind they were to relate to their neighbors in a godlike manner. Awareness of having been redeemed through God's love and grace would give the individual the capacity for extending God's love and mercy toward his neighbor. As God had treated them, so should they treat each other. If they really demonstrated love for their neighbors, the list of negatives would be irrelevant.

Thus, attitude of heart and mind was important in responding to neighbors. Revenge was to be avoided; vengeance belongs to God (v. 18; Deut. 32:34-46; cf. Rom. 12:19; Heb. 10:30). However, rebuke might be necessary so that "you will not share in his guilt" (v. 17; cf. 1 Tim. 4:12; 1 Pet. 2:23).

Although it is not explained, the prohibition against mating different kinds of animals (v. 19) may have had a preventative purpose, in view of orgiastic rites of Canaanite religious practices. Prohibiting mixture of different materials in garments may have expressed a concern for comfort, since some combinations can produce allergic reactions or static electricity.

In the moral realm, the covenantal law provided a slave girl with protection from the penalty of adultery if her master slept with her when she was assigned to another man. Adultery was considered a serious offense. However, since she was not free, the death penalty, which would have been normal for both parties (Deut. 22:23-24), was waived; but the man had to bring a ram, the costliest of offerings, as a reparation offering to obtain atonement for the sin of adultery (vv. 20-22).

Man was also to acknowledge God in his labors in planting fruit trees (vv. 23-25). Since little fruit would be produced during the first three years, it was not to be eaten. The fruit of the fourth year was to be offered to God as a holy praise offering. Beginning with the fifth year, one could freely enjoy the fruit provided through his efforts. Those instructions follow sound horticultural principles, which were also practiced by the Babylonians. But expressing appreciation to God for providing the fruit for their sustenance distinguished the people of Israel from the surrounding nations.

Certain pagan customs were explicitly forbidden (vv. 26-31). Eating meat with blood had already been forbidden (17:10-12). Now the Israelites were instructed that as God's people they should not participate in mechanical kinds of divination or soothsaying (v. 21). Nor were they to turn to mediums or spiritists (v. 31) who claimed to have contact with the spirits of the dead (cf. 1 Sam. 28:2-25). God had provided a way for them to know His will through the priests (Ex. 28:30; Lev. 8:8), and Moses, speaking for God, had assured them that they would be given other prophets (Deut. 18:14-22).

Bodily disfigurement as practiced in pagan mourning rites was prohibited (vv. 27-28), although mourning was not forbidden. Scarring or disfiguring the body, which God had created in His own image, was not appropriate for people identified with Him (cf. Deut. 14:1-2). In their bereavement they were to remember that He was "the LORD," with whom they had a vital relationship (v. 28; cf. 1 Thess. 4:13).

Temple prostitutes ("holy girls" in Hebrew) were usually associated with pagan shrines (cf. Deut. 23:17-18). The

Israelites were warned that cultic prostitution would fill the land with wickedness (v. 29). God's sanctuary was to be revered as the dwelling place of God among them, and Sabbaths were to be observed in recognition of God (v. 30). Such reverence for God would distinguish them as God's people (cf. Ezek. 23:38).

In human relations, the Israelites were to respect and honor the elderly (v. 32), as a way of revering God. Because within forty years after God had established His presence with them in the Tabernacle the entire generation over age twenty died in the wilderness, this emphasis upon reverence for God must have been most impressive. That generation had failed to revere God (Num. 13-14).

The Israelites were not to mistreat the alien among them but to "love him as yourself" (vv. 33-34). Having been aliens in Egypt, they were to remember that they had been redeemed by God and now should show God's love to the strangers among them.

In the marketplace and in business affairs they were to practice honesty in standards of length, weight, and quantity. They were accountable to God for the way in which they dealt with their fellow man. In all their relationships they were to be conscious that they belonged to God, "who brought you out of Egypt" (vv. 35-36). Further instructions given by Moses for conducting legal and business affairs are recorded in Deuteronomy 16:18-20; 25:13-15. Note that both Moses and the prophets condemned injustice (Deut. 25:16; Amos 8:5; Micah 6:10-11).

PENALTIES FOR DISOBEDIENCE (20:1-27)

The prohibitions and exhortations of chapter 20 may seem at first to be a repetition of those in the preceding chapter. But whereas certain patterns of behavior were explicitly forbidden (*apodictic* in form) in chapter 19, chapter 20 tells the consequences of breaking those laws (*casuistic* in form). In prescribing the ultimate punishment for breaking religious and family laws, these prohibitions reflect the sinfulness of the behavior so common to the surrounding cultures.

In Israel, the worst sin was to turn away from God to worship idols (vv. 2-5). To offer their children to Molech, the Moabite god, was to break the first and second commandments of the Decalogue. When God said, "I am the LORD your God," He expected exclusive devotion; to deviate from that relationship by turning to or acknowledging other gods merited the penalty of death. Anyone giving children to Molech "has defiled my sanctuary and profaned my holy name," said God (v. 3). He solemnly warned, "I will set my face against that man and his family and will cut off from their people both him and all who follow him in prostituting themselves to Molech" (v. 5). The same fate would befall those who turned to mediums and spiritists (vv. 6, 27).

Positive and constructive was the admonition that the Israelites consecrate, or sanctify, themselves and be holy "because I am the LORD your God . . . I am the LORD, who makes you holy" (vv. 7-8).

In contrast to laws of surrounding cultures, the priority in Israelite law was people, not property. Sins against family are delineated in verses 9-20. Family life was a priority. Parents represented the authority of God to the growing child and were to be accorded due honor, which the Decalogue taught was the first of duties toward others. To curse parents was not merely a matter of angry words but carried the idea "to make light of, despicable." It was equal to blasphemy. The death penalty was the maximum and not the minimum penalty and very likely was seldom, if ever, invoked (cf. Deut. 21:18-21).

The sexual sins listed in verses 10-21 disrupted family life. Repeatedly the death penalty is prescribed as the punishment for disregarding those prohibitions, emphasizing the importance of family life in Israel. Positively, it preserved the family structure in relation to God and undoubtedly provided a deterrent to sexual abuses that would destroy that relationship with God.

These decrees and laws were given in the context of the unique human-divine relationship between Israel and God

(vv. 22-27). If Israel conformed to the customs of the Canaanites, she would be subject to the fate of the Canaanites, and the land would "vomit you out" (v. 22). God's verdict on the Canaanites was, "I am going to drive [them] out before you. Because they did all these things, I abhorred them" (v. 23).

God had set Israel "apart from the nations to be my own" (v. 26) just as the Israelites were to set apart the clean from the unclean (chap. 11). They were to be holy in their pattern of living because God is holy.

The chapter concludes by again emphasizing the necessity for exclusive devotion to God, without deviation. Anyone who was a medium or spiritist was to be stoned. Although the Israelites were to love their neighbors, including the stranger and the sojourner, that love was not to include tolerance of idolatry but to call for those aliens to worship the God of Israel. Under no circumstances could anyone in the camp of Israel worship another god. For God's people there was no compromise, and anyone breaking the first commandment faced the penalty of death (cf. Deut. 13:1-10).

HOLINESS IN PRIESTLY SERVICE (21:1—22:33)

The ministry of the priesthood was essential to the Israelites' maintaining a vital relationship with God. Although the entire nation was God's "treasured possession," "a kingdom of priests and a holy nation" (Ex. 19:5-6), the priests, and especially the high priest, were in a special way to be set apart from the uncleanness common to the daily experiences of life.

Chapters 21 and 22 delineate the restrictions for the priests and for the ministry of bringing offerings to God. The priests were to exercise special care in avoiding uncleanness, which would disqualify them for officiating in worship at the sanctuary. It was their responsibility to keep from desecrating the sanctuary and profaning God's holy name. Positively, they were made holy through divine action. Six times in these chapters (21:8, 15, 23; 22:9, 16, 32) God declares that He is their sanctifier: "I am the LORD who makes you holy." That formula occurs in only one other place in Leviticus, in the appeal to the Israelites to consecrate themselves (20:8).

Because of their special responsibilities in officiating at the Tabernacle, the priests had several restrictions in their daily lives (vv. 1-9). They were to avoid all contact with the dead, except for close relatives, and were not to participate in mourning rites such as shaving the head (cf. 19:27-28) or defacing the body as the pagans did. Such was inappropriate for Israelite priests, because they presented "offerings made to the LORD by fire, the food of their God" (v. 6). Israel's God was holy, and His worship required honor that could not be demanded by the idols of the Canaanites.

Nor was a priest to marry a harlot or divorced woman. Cultic prostitution, so common in Canaanite shrines, had no place in the presence of a holy God. So offensive was the misuse of the human body in prostitution that a priest's daughter who indulged in immorality in Israel "must be burned in the fire" (v. 9).

The high priest was even more restricted. He was not allowed to come in contact with a dead body even in the burial of his parents, since that would render him unclean for seven days and interfere with his representing the Israelites at the sanctuary (cf. Num. 19:11-13). Nor was he to exhibit signs of mourning such as tearing his clothes or making his hair untidy.

In marriage the high priest was limited to "a virgin from his own people" (vv. 13-15). In addition to limiting his choice to someone from his own people, that rule also ensured that any child she bore was actually his own.

Physical defects that would prevent a member of a priestly family from officiating at a sacrifice are listed in verses 16-24. In divine service at the sanctuary physical normality and ceremonial holiness were closely associated. God's holiness required that which was normal and natural according to His creation. Israel's relationship with God had top priority, and the best, even in physical appearance, was essential when the priests represented God before the people and the people before God. Physical defects, however, did not make a priest unclean. As a member of the priestly family he was entitled to share the provision for the priests in the sacrificial meal (cf. Lev. 2:3, 10; 6:17-18).

Even though Aaron and his sons had been set apart and sanctified for service, they were solemnly reminded that they were vulnerable to ceremonial uncleanness each passing day (22:1-9). Such defilement could come from infectious skin disease, bodily discharge, contact with uncleanness, or eating unclean food. If they became unclean, they were not to participate in sacred offerings until they had undergone the prescribed procedure for cleansing. Priests were to set an example and heed these warnings lest they become guilty and face death in divine judgment.

As noted earlier, priests were entitled to a share of the offerings that were brought by the Israelites (Lev. 6-7). Since those offerings provided sustenance for the priest and his family, instructions were given to prevent abuse by relatives (22:10-16). The share in the offerings was for the priest's normal household, including slaves. Excluded from sharing in this food were hired workers and a married daughter, (although she could again be included if she were a widow or divorced, provided she were childless). If an unauthorized person mistakenly ate meat allotted to the priests, he had to make full restitution plus twenty percent.

In approaching God in worship, not only the priests but also the animals brought as offerings were required to be without defect (vv. 17-25; cf. chaps. 1-4). Stunted or deformed cows or sheep could be brought for freewill offerings but were not acceptable as a fulfillment of a vow (vv. 19-24). Castration of animals was forbidden (v. 24), and castrated animals, even if purchased from non-Israelites, were not acceptable for offerings (v. 25). Although no reason is given for that rule, castration obviously precluded the wholeness that was required in order for an offering to be accepted by God.

The restriction on killing animals (vv. 26-30) seems to be a deterrent to waste in the animal kingdom (cf. Deut. 22:6-7) as well as in nature (Deut. 20:19-20). Animals younger than eight days old were unacceptable for food or for offering to God.

Throughout chapters 21-22, the emphasis is on the priest's responsibility to stand between God and the Israelites at the sanctuary. They were to be ever vigilant in maintaining holiness and avoiding contact with uncleanness. At the same time, they were assured that it was God who made them holy and qualified them to come into His presence.

Instructions concerning the offerings were addressed to both the priests and the Israelites. The priests, by precept and example, were to impress on the Israelites a proper reverence in worshiping God. In that way God would be "acknowledged as holy by the Israelites" (v. 32). Among the nations that surrounded them, the Israelites were unique in having a vital relationship with God.

7

RELIGIOUS FESTIVALS

LEVITICUS 23:1—24:55

Religious festivals were very important in the Israelites' maintaining their relationship with God. Addressed to the laity, chapters 23-24 delineate the observances significant for the Israelites throughout the year. Those festivals are designated as feasts appointed by the Lord (vv. 2, 3, 37, 44) and as sacred assemblies (vv. 2, 4, 7-8, 21, 24, 27, 35, 37). They were set times when the Israelites assembled at the sanctuary to meet with God. Repeatedly the Israelites were instructed to "do no regular work" on those days of sacred assembly (vv. 7-8, 21, 25, 28, 30-31, 36).

This calendar for religious assemblies provided guidance for the priests, who probably passed it on to the laity as they instructed the Israelites. The offerings are briefly identified as offerings "made to the LORD by fire" (vv. 8, 13, 18, 25, 27, 36-37). Numbers 28-29 gives more specific details for the priests, who were responsible to guide the laity in bringing the proper offerings for each sacred assembly.

The three great celebrations during the year were the Feasts of Passover, Weeks, and Tabernacles (Ex. 23:14-19; 34:18-24; Deut. 16:1-17). Following is the religious calendar:

First month, *Abib* or *Nisan* (April)

   14—Passover (Lev. 23:5; Ex. 12:1-51; Num. 28:16-25; Deut. 16:1-8).

   15—Feast of Unleavened Bread (Lev. 23:6-8; Ex. 13:1-10, 23:14-15)

   —Sheaf of Firstfruits (Lev. 23:9-14)

Third month, *Siwan* (June)
  6—Feast of Weeks (Lev. 23:15-22; Ex. 34:22; Num. 28:26-31; Deut. 16:9-12)
  —Feast of Harvest (Ex. 23:16)
  —Day of Firstfruits (Num. 28:26)
Seventh month, *Tishri* (October)
  1—Feast of Trumpets (Lev. 23:25; Num. 29:1-6)
  10—Day of Atonement (Lev. 23:26-32; 16:1-34; Num. 29:7-11)
  15—Feast of Tabernacles (Booths) (Lev. 23:33-43; Num. 29:12-38; Deut. 16:13-17)
  —Feast of Ingathering (Ex. 23:16; 34:22)

The first Passover was observed on the eve of Israel's departure from Egypt (Ex. 12). The second Passover was celebrated at Mount Sinai, one year after the Exodus (Num. 9:1-14). The Tabernacle was dedicated on the first day of the first month (*Nisan*) and was the center of the Passover observance on the first anniversary of the deliverance from Egypt, on the fourteenth day of *Abib*. Israelites who were ceremonially unclean on that day could celebrate on the fourteenth day of the second month.

On the twentieth day of the second month the Israelites broke camp and in eleven days reached Kadesh-barnea (Num. 10:11; Deut. 1:2). Very likely they did not again observe the annual festivals under Moses while they marked time in the wilderness during the next thirty-eight years. The next recorded observance of the Passover took place under Joshua, at Gilgal in the land of Canaan (Josh. 5:10-12).

The instructions in chapter 23 were given in anticipation of the Israelites' living in the land of Canaan. The observances of the three primary festivals are related to the harvesting of grain and fruits throughout the year. Sheaves of barley were presented as firstfruits the day after the Passover. Bread of the firstfruits, made from wheat, was offered at the Feast of Weeks in the third month. After all the crops of grain and fruit were harvested came the Feast of Tabernacles, also called the Feast of Ingathering.

Appropriately, in his last appeal to the Israelites on the plains of Moab before his death, Moses reminded the new generation to observe these holidays (Deut. 16:1-17).

THE SABBATH (23:1-4)

The Sabbath was the primary sacred assembly for the Israelites as God's people (23:1-4). Every seventh day was to be observed as "a day of sacred assembly . . . wherever you live" (v. 3).

For the Israelites, observing the weekly Sabbath became a practical reality en route to Mount Sinai from Egypt (Ex. 16-17). In need of sustenance, they received a miraculous daily supply of manna, with a double portion to gather on the sixth day. But none was provided on the seventh day, which God had designated as "a day of rest" (Ex. 16:23). They were taught, "The LORD has given you the sabbath" (Ex. 16:29). Since they were no longer working for the Egyptians and there was no manna to gather on the seventh day, the Israelites "rested on the seventh day" (16:30). It is not likely that the Israelites would have been allowed to observe the Sabbath as a day of rest in servitude in Egypt. This is the first recorded observance of the Sabbath in the history of mankind.

When the law was given at Mount Sinai, the Israelites were instructed to "remember the sabbath day by keeping it holy. . . . [and] not do any work," because God had rested on the seventh day after six days of creative activity (Ex. 20:8-11). Subsequently God instructed Moses, "The Israelites are to observe the Sabbath, celebrating it for the generations to come as a lasting covenant. It will be a sign between me and the Israelites forever" (Ex. 31:16-17). When Moses repeated that commandment on the plains of Moab forty years later, the Israelites were reminded to keep the Sabbath holy in remembrance of their having been rescued from Egyptian bondage (Deut. 5:14-15). Every Sabbath they were to remember that God had created their nation and that they were dependent on God.

The Israelites were to recognize the Sabbath as the Lord's own day, and to rest from work. God, who hallowed this day, was to be worshiped as the Author of covenant mercies and the Sustainer of Israel.

On the Sabbath, additional offerings were presented at the Tabernacle. As discussed earlier, a burnt offering of one lamb, accompanied by appropriate grain and drink offerings, was offered every day, morning and evening, for the nation of Israel (Ex. 29:38-43). On the Sabbath, that offering was doubled (Num. 28:9, 19).

Israel was unique among the nations in her observance of every seventh day as a holy day, so designated by divine revelation. The entire nation of Israel observed the Sabbath; in contrast it is interesting to note that in the Babylonian culture, certain classes in society observed five days a month (the seventh, fourteenth, nineteenth, twenty-first, and the twenty-eighth) as sabbaths in hopes of appeasing their gods and averting their wrath through special offerings. The Israelites came to God in worship with the keen realization that God had redeemed them out of Egyptian bondage. They were assured that by proper observance of the Sabbath they would "know that I am the LORD, who makes you holy" (Ex. 31:12-13).

In the Christian faith, the relationship between the Lord's Day (Rev. 1:10), the first day of the week (Matt. 28:1; Mark 16:2), and the resurrection of Jesus Christ is analogous to the relationship between the Sabbath and Israel's Exodus from Egypt. For the Israelites, the Exodus marked God's creation of a new nation (Ex. 15:13). For the Christian, the resurrection power released through faith in Christ (Eph. 1:19) marks the beginning of a liberated life (Eph. 2:4-10).

The principle behind the commandment to observe the Sabbath day applies to the Christian's observance of the first day of the week. A day of rest should be a time devoted to thanksgiving for divine deliverance and to recognizing our total dependence upon God. As a new creation, the Israelite nation (Deut. 5:15) and Christians, new creatures in Christ

(2 Cor. 5:17), celebrate the first creation (Ex. 20:11) when they set aside one day in seven as a day of rest, holy unto the Lord.

By observing the Sabbath, the Israelites distinguished their religion from the religions of neighboring nations. By observing the Lord's Day, Christians distinguish themselves from a culture where God is not acknowledged or honored.[1]

THE PASSOVER (23:5-14)

The most important annual festival was the Passover (v. 5). The rites and ceremonies of this festival had been vividly impressed upon the Israelites on the night of their departure from Egypt (Ex. 12). Passover was observed on the fourteenth evening of the first month, in the spring of the year (*Nisan,* April). This annual observance reminded the Israelites that the blood of the lamb applied to the doorposts of each family home had saved them from divine judgment.

Beginning with the fifteenth day of Nisan, they were to eat unleavened bread for seven days (vv. 6-8). Eating bread without yeast served as a reminder that when God had delivered them from slavery, they had had to leave Egypt suddenly, allowing no time to leaven bread. The details for observing the feast are given in Numbers 28:16-25.

An offering of firstfruits was presented the day after the Passover began (vv. 9-14). This was the beginning of the barley harvest, the first grain to ripen in Palestine. A sheaf was brought to the priest, who waved it before the Lord and offered a burnt offering of a year-old lamb, an offering of grain, and a drink offering of wine. Acknowledging God as the giver of the crop, the Israelite could then enjoy the grain himself.

THE FEAST OF WEEKS (PENTECOST) (23:15-22)

The Feast of Weeks was also called the Feast of Harvest (Ex. 23:16), and it marked the end of the grain or wheat

---

1. P. C. Craigie, *The Book of Deuteronomy* (Grand Rapids: Eerdmans, 1976), pp. 156-58.

harvest. It was a one-day celebration observed fifty days after the sheaf of the first grain (barley) was presented at the sanctuary on the second day of Passover. In the New Testament, this feast was called Pentecost (Acts 2:1), from the Greek word for "fiftieth."

On this day, "an offering of new grain" consisting of two loaves baked with yeast was waved before the Lord as an offering of firstfruits. Consequently this feast was also known as the "day of firstfruits" (Num. 28:26-31). The animal sacrifices prescribed for this day were more elaborate than those for the Feast of Unleavened Bread.

For the Israelites, offering firstfruits after they arrived in Canaan would be a new experience, since they had not been an agricultural people and thus had had no harvest festivals. After possessing the land, the offering of firstfruits would inaugurate the new life that for so long they had anticipated on the basis of God's promises. The ceremony Moses prescribed for this occasion is delineated in Deuteronomy 26:1-11. With this feast marking the beginning of his new life, the Israelite would confess that he had been in bondage in Egypt, had been delivered by God, and had been brought into the Promised Land through God's power. Presenting the firstfruits, he worshiped God and rejoiced in His goodness.

Appropriately, the Israelites were instructed to leave the edges of the fields and the gleanings "for the poor and the aliens" (Lev. 23:22). This one-day sacred assembly was to be a time of rejoicing for everyone—"you, your sons and daughters, your menservants and maidservants, the Levites in your towns, and the aliens, the fatherless and the widows living among you. Remember that you were slaves in Egypt, and follow carefully these decrees" (Deut. 16:9-12).

How much were the Israelites to give from the crops that would grow for them in the land of Canaan? Instead of giving legalistic instructions, Moses simply stated that the Israelites should "celebrate the Feast of Weeks to the LORD your God by giving a freewill offering in proportion to the blessings the LORD your God has given you" (Deut. 16:10). Centuries later the apostle Paul, following that pattern, exhorted the Corinthian Christians to give as God had prospered, or "in keeping with his income" (1 Cor. 16:2).

Throughout the year as crops of barley, wheat, grapes, olives, and other produce ripened, the firstfruits were to be brought to the sanctuary for the Levites and the priests (cf. Ex. 23:19; 34:22-26; Lev. 2:14-16; Num. 18:12; Deut. 18:4). In that manner, sustenance was provided for the priests and those who were serving at the sanctuary.

THE FEAST OF TABERNACLES (23:23-44)

The third great festival, the Feast of Tabernacles, marked the climax of the religious year with an eight-day celebration, from the fifteenth to the twenty-first of the seventh month, *Tishri*. The seventh month was ushered in on the first day by a sacred assembly and by trumpet blasts, designating it as a sacred month. On the tenth day another sacred assembly was held and atonement was made for the nation of Israel. Five days later began a week-long celebration of rejoicing and giving thanks for the harvest God had provided.

The Feast of Trumpets was observed in a sacred assembly, and the sounding of trumpets announced the cessation of labor (Lev. 23:23-25). In addition to the daily sacrifices (Ex. 28:38-43), the Israelites were to offer burnt offerings with grain and drink offerings, as well as a sin offering, to make atonement (Num. 29:1-6). At the close of the agricultural season, this solemn day of rest ushered in the month in which were observed two special occasions vitally important in their relationship with God.

Verses 26-32 briefly describe the laity's observance of the Day of Atonement. They were admonished to abstain from work and to "deny," or afflict, themselves (vv. 27, 29, 32). It was a day of humiliation. Although there is no explicit Scriptural command to fast on the day, the Israelites' penitential exercise may have included fasting. In bringing the prescribed offerings and assembling in an attitude of contrition and humility, the Israelites were assured on that day the proper atonement was made for all their sins of accident and omission (cf. Lev. 16:1-34).

The Feast of Tabernacles (vv. 33-44) was one of the most joyous occasions of the year. Since it marked the end of the harvest season, it was also called the Feast of Ingathering (Ex. 23:16; 34:22). During this eight-day celebration, *Tishri* 15-21, the Israelites lived in booths made from the foliage of beautiful trees, palm branches, leafy boughs, and willows from river banks. In festive rejoicing the Israelites were to reenact their redemption from Egypt and their living in tents en route to Canaan. It was a time of joy for the entire family and community. Sons, daughters, servants, Levites, aliens, fatherless, and widows were to celebrate and rejoice in the produce they had harvested. Acknowledging God as the One who had blessed the work of their hands, they were assured that their joy would "be complete" (Deut. 16:13-15).

The first and eighth days of the feast were to be days of rest. The offerings prescribed during this week were elaborate and expensive (Num. 29:12-40). They were in addition to the offerings presented each day throughout the year. In addition, people brought gifts, freewill offerings, and whatever they had vowed.

These three great festivals—Passover, the Feast of Weeks, and the Feast of Tabernacles—brought to each generation of Israelites a renewed consciousness of God. Recalling at Passover that they had been slaves in Egypt, they realized afresh that God's mighty acts had freed them and sustained them through the wilderness journey. As they presented their firstfruits at the Feast of Weeks they acknowledged that it was God who had given them the land of Canaan and provided their sustenance. As they shared the produce of the land with others at the Feast of Tabernacles, they acknowledged God's abundant blessings.

Moses warned members of the new generation, in light of their parents' failures (Deut. 1-4), to give thanks to God as they came to these sacred festivals. "No man should appear before the LORD emptyhanded: Each of you must bring a gift

in proportion to the way the LORD your God has blessed you''
(Deut. 16:16-17).

FESTIVAL CONTINUITY

How do the Israelite festivals relate to New Testament
times? Is there in this calendar of sacred assemblies a continuity between the testaments?

The Passover took on a new significance in God's fuller
revelation through the death and resurrection of Christ. Paul
asserted, "Christ, our Passover Lamb, has been sacrificed"
(1 Cor. 5:7; cf. John 1:29).

Christ died in the Passover season. Before His death He
partook of the Passover meal with His disciples (Matt. 26:17;
Luke 22:7-16) and told them that He was about to die. John's
account of the crucifixion refers to the fact that Jesus' bones
were not broken and quotes from the Passover account in Exodus (John 19:14, 36; cf. Ex. 12:46). In this way John identifies Jesus with the paschal lamb.

Jesus rose from the dead on the day after the Sabbath, the
day on which the Israelites presented the sheaves of grain as
firstfruits at the sanctuary. Jesus had represented himself as a
grain of wheat falling into the ground and dying in order to
produce many seeds (John 12:24). Paul speaks of Christ, in
His resurrection, as the firstfruits and the basis of our hope of
resurrection.

Consequently, it is fitting that those who have a vital relationship with God should celebrate the death and resurrection
of Christ on Good Friday and Easter. The Israelites as a nation were redeemed from Egyptian bondage when they believed in God (Ex. 4:31; 14:31) and, in obedience, offered a
lamb through whose blood they were spared divine judgment.
In like manner, the individual who believes in Christ will not
come under judgment but has the assurance of eternal life
(John 3:16-18). As the sheaf of grain presented to God expressed the Israelites' hope for harvest, so Christ's resurrection assures those who believe in Him of their own future
resurrection.

The Feast of Weeks, fifty days after the presentation of the sheaf of grain, was called Pentecost in New Testament times (Acts 2:1). The Israelites' offering of firstfruits at this one-day celebration represented the harvest of wheat. After Christ's resurrection, the thousands turning to Him on Pentecost, when the Holy Spirit was miraculously manifested, were also firstfruits (James 1:18), the beginning of an ingathering that will continue to the end of this age (cf. John 12:24).

The celebration of the Feast of Tabernacles at the end of the harvest season was one of rejoicing before the Lord, expressed through abundant giving from one's crops and sharing in fellowship with one's family and the entire community. Expressions of thankfulness and rejoicing in giving and sharing characteristic of the Feast of Tabernacles should be part of the pattern of living of all those today who acknowledge the abundant provisions of God.

Through observing their festivals, the Israelites maintained a keen awareness of God's involvement in both the material and the spiritual aspects of life. That awareness is just as important for us. Note the following parallels:

1. By observing every seventh day as a day holy unto the Lord and by ceasing from work, we, like the Israelites, express thanks to God for His power, which obtained our liberation and continues to sustain us.
2. The Hebrew Passover provided an annual opportunity to instruct members of each generation concerning their deliverance through the blood of the paschal lamb and their covenant relationship with God. For Christians, the Lord's Supper focuses on Christ as the sacrificial Lamb (cf. Isa. 53) through whose blood we have redemption. By observing the Lord's Supper we renew our consciousness of our deliverance from the bondage of sin through the death of Jesus Christ.
3. In bringing the firstfruits, the Israelites acknowledged God as the source of the produce of the land. Paul tells us that Christ's resurrection made Him the firstfruits from the

dead (1 Cor. 15:20-23) and thus the source of our hope of resurrection.

4. The Day of Atonement made the Israelites conscious of the cleansing and forgiveness of sin that enabled them to have a relationship with God. Although that day's priestly ceremony at the sanctuary has become obsolete through the atoning work of Christ, we do well to remind ourselves of our own atonement and to worship God in contrition and humility.

5. On the joyous occasion of Pentecost, the entire nation gave thanks to God, especially for material provisions. By offering God loaves of bread, animal sacrifices, and gifts of grain, they expressed their thanksgiving for God's care in every area of life. We should remember that God provides sunshine and rain for all (Matt. 10:45), but the gift of the Holy Spirit is only for those who ask (Luke 11:13). The Feast of Pentecost was the eventful day on which the Holy Spirit came upon the early church (Acts 2:1-4).

6. The Feast of Tabernacles was another joyous celebration in which the Israelites recalled their wanderings in the wilderness and God's goodness in providing for them. In gratitude they shared material things with the needy among them. That expression of gratitude and joyous sharing with the less fortunate should also be a vital part of our relationship with God.

CARE AND REVERENCE FOR THE HOLY (24:1-23)

Chapter 24 covers two topics. Verses 1-9 provide instructions for care of the Tabernacle lamps and the weekly supply of bread for the priests, which supplemented the offering of bread as firstfruits (23:17) and the grain offering (23:37). Verses 10-23 recount an incident of blasphemy, which may have occurred shortly after the instructions for supplying the oil and bread were given.

The lampstand, made of pure gold (Ex. 25:31-39), was located in the forepart of the Holy Place of the Tabernacle (Ex. 37:17-24; 40:24-25). Aaron and his sons had been assigned the responsibility of maintaining the lamps, supplying them with "clear oil from pressed olives" brought by the Israelites (Ex. 27:20-21).

Those instructions are repeated in Leviticus 24, stressing the importance of that responsibility in that those lamps furnished light for the Holy Place. Daily the oil had to be replenished and the wicks trimmed. Although Aaron was the first to light the lamps after the Tabernacle was erected (Num. 8:1-3), the responsibility was shared by other priests, since the lamps were to be kept burning continually, "for generations to come" (Lev. 24:3).

In the Holy Place, a table was placed on the right side, opposite the lampstand, which was located on the left side. On that table, made of acacia wood and overlaid with pure gold (Ex. 25:23-30; 37:10-16), was placed the supply of bread called "the bread of the Presence" (Ex. 25:30). Plates, ladles, bowls, and pitchers used for pouring drink offerings (Ex. 37:16) were also placed on that table.

Every Sabbath, twelve loaves of bread were to be placed in two rows on that table. Although Scripture does not say so, the twelve loaves may have represented the twelve tribes of Israel (cf. the ephod, on which twelve stones represented the twelve tribes, Ex. 28:9-12).

The episode of the blasphemer publicly stoned for cursing God (vv. 10-23) provides interesting case law in the life of Israel. Very likely the incident occured soon after Moses had given instructions for the observance of the feasts and seasons and for the care of the Holy Place. The drastic penalty for cursing reinforced awareness of the holiness of God as He dwelt among His people in the camp of Israel.

The sin in question, committed by the son of an Israelite mother and an Egyptian father, was blaspheming "the name of the LORD with a curse" (v. 11; cf. v. 16). In this context "the name" (v. 16) speaks of God's character and identity as the one who had promised deliverance for the Israelites (Ex. 3:15). The blasphemer was guilty of using God's name in a curse, which had been explicitly forbidden (Ex. 22:28).

Until this incident, the penalty for cursing God had not been prescribed, so the man was arrested and placed in custody to await divine revelation. That he was to be executed by stoning was not Moses' decision but the judgment of God. The penalty for the blasphemy involved those who heard it as well as the blasphemer (vv. 13-16). The hearers laid their hands on the blasphemer's head, identifying him as guilty, and took him outside the camp to be stoned by the community. The heap of stones was a continual reminder to the community of the crime of cursing God. That this penalty for blasphemy became normative in Israel is evidenced by the execution of Naboth, falsely accused of blasphemy under Jezebel (1 Kings 21:10, 13).

Any individual, whether a native Israelite or a foreigner, was expected to show respect for God. The person guilty of cursing and blasphemy was responsible to bear his own punishment (vv. 15-16). (Enforcement of this law continued into New Testament times. Both Jesus [Matt. 26:65-66] and Stephen [Acts 6:11-14; 7:57-58] were accused of blasphemy and condemned to death.)

Verses 17-23 cite a series of cases to illustrate the principle that punishment must match the offense. It is one of three passages projecting the *lex talionis,* a law that prescribes punishment proportional to the crime (cf. Ex. 21:23-25; Deut. 19:21).

"Fracture for fracture, eye for eye, tooth for tooth" (Lev. 24:20) may express the ancient Semitic legal formula of *lex talionis.* Since it signified public justice it may have averted blood-feuds and other forms of private revenge. It stated the limits of retribution for specific offenses; it probably was seldom applied literally.[2]

In the Old Testament code of law as well as in the laws of the Mesopotamian culture, the death penalty was applied to a wider spectrum of crimes than in modern Western juris-

---

2. R. K. Harrison, *Leviticus* (Downers Grove, Ill.: Inter-Varsity, 1980), pp. 222-23.

prudence. In the code of Hammurabi, property was often considered more important than person; property offenses such as theft were capital crimes. In Israelite law, sins against the family and religion were most serious. A person was so important that "life for life" was required (v. 17; cf. Gen. 9:5-6). Although restitution was required when an individual stole or killed an animal (v. 18, 21; cf. Ex. 22:1, 4), there was no material compensation for murder (Num. 35:29-31). Premeditated murder, like blasphemy, was a capital crime.

In teaching about the fulfillment of the law, Jesus quoted the *lex talionis* (Matt. 5:17-47) and criticized, not the law itself, but the legalistic interpretation current in His day. He may have been attacking those who had turned "this legalistic principle into a maxim for personal conduct" in a pattern of self-righteous living,[3] showing a concern for personal behavior and attitudes.

He did not denounce the administration of justice through the courts of law; His life exemplified an attitude of respect for those entrusted with authority and responsibility for governing the land.

Subsequent New Testament teaching supports the principle that judges and rulers are responsible to mete out punishment appropriate to the crime (Rom. 13:4; 1 Pet. 2:14).

THE SABBATICAL YEAR (25:1-55)

The concluding instructions concerning the Israelites' religious observances focus attention upon the land and the economic and social aspects of living in Canaan. Chapter 25 prescribes a sabbath rest for the land every seven years and a year of jubilee every fiftieth year, when all land would revert to its original owners and all Israelites who had committed themselves to servitude would be released to return to their own clans and families.

Throughout this chapter, the relationship between God and

---

3. Gordon J. Wenham, *The Book of Leviticus* (Grand Rapids: Eerdmans, 1979), p. 313.

the Israelites is foundational. Note this emphasis throughout the chapter:

"I am the LORD your God" (vv. 17, 38, 55)

"who brought you out of Egypt" (vv. 38, 42, 55)

"to give you the land of Canaan" (vv. 1, 38)

"the Israelites are my servants" (vv. 42, 55)

"to fear and revere God in obedience" (vv. 17, 36, 43).

The observance of the sabbatical year and the year of jubilee are directly related to the weekly Sabbath observance. As a nation freed from bondage, the Israelites observed the Sabbath as a day of rest and freedom from work (Ex. 16:1-36). Manna was supplied for six days with a double portion on the sixth to provide for the seventh. That kind of miraculous supply was promised to them for their future in Canaan. They were assured that every sixth year they would have an abundant crop, sufficient to meet their needs during the seventh year and the jubilee year, when the land would be allowed to rest.

After settling in Canaan the Israelites were to allow the land to "observe a sabbath to the LORD," the sabbatical year (25:1-7). They were reminded that it was the land God had given them (v. 2). They were the recipients of God's gift; consequently, they had stewardship responsibility to God. For six years they could sow and harvest, reap and produce, but the seventh year was to be a time of rest for the land. During that year the vineyards and orchards were to remain unattended and the land allowed to lie fallow. The sabbatical growth that grew of itself was not to be harvested by the owner. It "will be food for you—for yourself, your manservant and maidservant, and the hired worker and temporary resident who live among you, as well as for your livestock and the wild animals in your land" (vv. 6-7).

That provision was especially important to the poor. Out of the abundance that God provided during the sabbatical year, the poor and needy were allowed to harvest for themselves (Ex. 23:10-11). Note that even beasts were provided for.

Thus every seven years the whole nation of Israel, landowners as well as the less fortunate servants, workers, and aliens, were made conscious anew that God had given them the land. By allowing the land a sabbath rest, the Israelites acknowledged that it was God's gift to them, and in obedience they recognized God as the owner. By allowing the poor to eat what God caused to grow when the land was not tended by the owner, they acknowledged anew that God cared for the needy among them, and by obeying this instruction they practiced the principle of giving and sharing with the less fortunate.

After living forty-nine years in the land and observing seven sabbatical years, they were to observe the fiftieth year as the year of jubilee (25:8-55). The jubilee year was announced on the Day of Atonement, with the blast of a trumpet, or ram's horn, called a *yobel,* roughly transliterated "jubilee." (The word *jubilee* probably comes from the root word *yabal,* meaning "to bring [forth]," referring to the bringing forth of produce. The Septuagint translates it "release."[4]) With that blast came the proclamation of freedom for everyone to return to his property and to his family. In addition, the jubilee year was also to be observed as a fallow year for the land.

Land had to be returned to its original owners (vv. 13-17). The land had been allotted to the tribes when they entered Canaan, and it was not to be transferred (Num. 32; 36:9; Josh. 13-19). The earth belonged to God (Ex. 9:29), who had promised to give the land of Canaan to the Israelites (Gen. 15:7; 17:8; 24:7; Ex. 6:4; Lev. 20:24; 25:2, 38; Deut. 5:16). Consequently the Israelites were tenants and were to acknowledge that God held the title to the land on which they lived.

Because all land reverted to its original owner in the year of jubilee, the price paid for any given piece of land would be proportionate to the years remaining in the forty-nine-year cycle. Respect and reverence for God, the owner of the land,

---

4. R. North, *Sociology of the Biblical Jubilee* (Rome: Pontifical Biblical Institute, 1954), pp. 96-97.

would temper any attempt at exploiting one another in such a business transaction.

The Israelites were assured of God's provision if they obeyed His instructions (vv. 18-22). In observing the jubilee year, they faced two years during which the land was idle. But they were given the divine promise that they would have a miraculously abundant crop in the year before those two years to sustain them until the crop of the following year would be available.

The Israelites to whom Moses gave these instructions had received a double supply of manna every sixth day in the wilderness to sustain them through the seventh, when none was available for them to gather. Consequently they had experience on which to base their faith that God would miraculously provide for them when they allowed the land to be fallow even two years in succession in order to observe the year of jubilee.

Land was not to be sold permanently since "the land is mine and you are but aliens and my tenants" (vv. 23-28). If someone, because of unfortunate circumstances or poverty, had to sell his land, it was expected that a near relative would aid in redeeming it (cf. Ruth 4; Jer. 32). If no one could aid him and he could not repurchase it himself, then he would have to wait for the year of jubilee, when he would receive it back.

Houses in walled cities did not revert to the original owners in the jubilee year. The right to repurchase a house inside a walled city expired one year after the sale. But houses located outside walled cities, very likely on farm or pasture land, were under the jubilee year provisions (vv. 29-35). Houses allotted to the Levites in forty-eight cities throughout the land (Num. 35:1-8; Josh. 21:1-42) reverted to the original owners during the year of jubilee if they had been sold during the forty-nine-year period. The pasture land allotted to the Levites could not be sold.

Charging interest for money lent to a fellow Israelite was prohibited (vv. 35-38; cf. Deut. 23:19-20). Israel's society in

Canaan was not based on a complex financial and commercial structure as ours is. The Israelites did not buy the land but were to conquer and occupy it, accepting it as God's gift to them. Since loans were usually made because of extreme poverty, to charge interest would aggravate the crisis that had necessitated the loan in the first place.

It was considered improper for a wealthy Israelite to lend money or sell food to a fellow Israelite at a profit. By foregoing interest and profit he would show his reverence for God, acknowledging that God had given him his wealth. He was to be as generous to his fellow Israelite as God had been to him.

An Israelite who was unable to pay a debt could choose to sell himself as a servant in lieu of payment (vv. 39-43). His period of service was normally limited to six years (Ex. 21:2; Deut. 15:12), but he was released in the jubilee year if that occurred before the six-year period was complete.

The Israelite who bought him was to treat him as a hired man and not as a slave. He was not to treat this servant ruthlessly but accord him the dignity of a brother. In the divine-human relationship, all Israelites were God's servants (v. 42) and were equal before God. Reverence for God, who had brought all the Israelites out of Egypt to be His servants, would not allow ruthless treatment of a fellow Israelite. The master was also responsible for the care of the servant's immediate family members. Those provisions were designed to preserve the dignity and humanity of the debtor without allowing him to evade his social and financial responsibilities.

Non-Israelites could be bought and sold as slaves (vv. 44-46). They could be passed on to the next generation as property. Although they were not included in the jubilee release, it should be noted that they had the religious rights and privileges of the Sabbath rest (Ex. 20:10; 23:12). They could also participate in the religious feasts of the Israelites if they were circumcised (Ex. 12:43-45). A slave belonging to a priest was allowed to eat the sacred offering (22:10-12, a privilege denied to the priest's married daughter or a hired servant or alien).

The slavery of the Old Testament economy is not to be compared to the slavery practiced by the Greeks and Romans during the closing centuries of the Old Testament era. An Israelite who owned a slave tempered his treatment of that slave by his reverence for God. The Old Testament law also protected a slave from inhumane treatment. Anyone murdering a slave was subject to execution (Ex. 21:12), and anyone abusing a slave was to be punished (Ex. 21:20-21). If a slave was maimed, even in the loss of one tooth, he was to be set free (Ex. 21:26-27).

If an Israelite sold himself to an alien or a temporary resident, he retained the right of redemption (vv. 47-53). That would allow any willing relative to pay his debt and restore him to freedom. The price of redemption was proportional to the number of years remaining before the jubilee year. The non-Israelite was also warned not to rule over the Israelite with severity but to treat him as a hired servant.

The chapter closes with a reiteration of the provison that in the year of jubilee, release was at hand for anyone who had been subjected to bondage (vv. 54-55). That jubilee observance for Israel was based on the principle that no Israelite could be in perpetual bondage because he was a child of God (Deut. 14:1). God had brought them out of Egypt and declared, "The Israelites belong to me as servants. They are my servants. . . . I am the LORD your God" (v. 55).

When Moses spoke to his people on the plains of Moab before he died, he appealed to them on the basis of the principle that they should love God and their fellow man, a humanitarian principle demonstrated in the jubilee year observance. Israel's existence as an independent nation was a result of God's redeeming love and action; Moses addressed the Israelites as "children of the LORD your God" (Deut. 14:1).

Repeatedly Moses appealed to them to love God exclusively

and wholeheartedly (Deut. 1:11; note especially 6:4; 10:12).
God's love reached back to the patriarchs (Deut. 4:37) and
was manifested in the people's miraculous redemption when
Moses led them out of Egyptian bondage (Ex. 12-14). Just as
in observing the annual feasts they acknowledged God as
their deliverer and sustainer, so in observing the sabbatical
year and the year of jubilee they acknowledged God as the
giver of the land. They reflected His generosity to them in
sharing the produce with the poor, granting freedom to those
in servitude, and returning land to its original owners.

The laws of the sabbatical year and the year of jubilee
demonstrate that an equitable society has to be grounded in
moral and spiritual principles. The humanitarian and social
justice proposed in this chapter dictate middle course between
the extremes of rampant Communism and unrestricted
capitalism. Each Israelite was assured of individual freedom
and the right to the land entrusted to him as God's gift. He
was assured that under Israelite law he could retain his
ancestral holdings. In later years, Ahab very likely recognized
this but allowed Jezebel to command the execution of Naboth
in order that he might have Naboth's vineyard (1 Kings 21.)

Before his death, Moses emphasized this social justice
(Deut. 12-30). God's love for the Israelites was to be reflected
in their relationships with one another. Love for neighbor
issued out of wholehearted, exclusive love for God.

The proclamation of "liberty throughout the land to all its
inhabitants" (25:10) normally would occur once in a person's
lifetime. How often it was actually observed during Old
Testament times is difficult to ascertain. The only reference to
a release proclamation in the history of Israel occurred under
Zedekiah when Jerusalem was besieged by the Babylonians in
586 B.C. (Jer. 34:8-17). When the siege was lifted the people
profaned God's name by reclaiming the slaves they had
released. Subsequently Jeremiah announced God's judgment
in abandoning them "to fall by the sword, plague, and
famine" (Jer. 34:17).

Isaiah announced a proclamation of liberty, or "freedom

for the captives'' (61:1). Jesus read that passage from Isaiah in a synagogue in Nazareth and announced that He had come to fulfill it (Luke 4:18-21). That may be the basis of Paul's anticipation of the liberation of creation from bondage into the "glorious freedom of the children of God" (Rom. 8:21).

8

SOLEMN CHOICES

LEVITICUS 26:1—27:34

The unique covenantal relationship between the Israelites and God described in Leviticus 26 gives a long-range perspective for the centuries after they had settled in Canaan. The emphasis is upon maintaining their vital relationship with God, with the alternatives realistically set forth. Blessings and God's favor awaited them if they maintained their reverence for God. Curses and destruction would overtake them if they turned away from Him. A vow was a voluntary commitment to God that was to be honored (chap. 27).

BLESSINGS AND CURSES (26:1-46)

In literary structure, the blessings and curses of Leviticus 26 are similar to those found in treaties of the Hittites, Assyrians, and Arameans during the second millennium B.C. Often the treaties between a conquering suzerain and a conquered vassal concluded with a series of threats and promises, depending upon observance of the treaty. Usually the curses outnumbered the blessings.

Although there are similarities in literary pattern and context, there are also unique differences. Similar to the conclusion in this chapter in Leviticus are Exodus 23:25-33, Deuteronomy 28:1-68, and Joshua 24:20.

The unique relationship between God and Israel is distinctly set forth in the opening statement (26:1-2).

I am the LORD your God, therefore:
•do not make or worship idols,

126

• observe My sabbaths,
• reverence My sanctuary.

The identification of God, though often repeated (cf. Lev. 19:2-3, 13, 36-37), is fundamentally important in this context (26:1-2, 44-45). Whereas in secular treaties curses were uttered in the names of many gods, and prayers were addressed to deities with the superstitious belief that those gods could aid them, the text here identifies Israel's God as the one who brought them "out of Egypt in the sight of the nations to be their God" (v. 45). God had already displayed His might in setting them free to be His people.

That God would also give them the land of Canaan, which He had promised to Abraham, Isaac, and Jacob (v. 42). Basic to the blessings and curses is the fulfillment of that promise. Israel's God, in aiding His people to conquer and possess the land of Canaan, would be uniquely distinguished from the gods of the Canaanites, who would be dispossessed. Their gods would not help them, no matter how much they prayed.

The first of three basic laws the Israelites needed to heed in order to enjoy God's blessings was not to worship other gods. That negative command must be considered in the cultural and religious context of Canaan, where there were many gods, idols, and shrines. The Israelites were forbidden to make idols of cast metal (non-existent things, Lev. 19:4); graven images; sacred stones that were cultic representations of deities (Ex. 20:4); or carved, decorated sacred stones (pillars representing El or Baal, the two principal Canaanite deities).

God demanded that the Israelites worship Him exclusively. A basic break in the God-Israelite relationship was at risk any time an Israelite bowed down to worship another god. Thus this warning was extremely important. It was for that reason that the Israelites were commanded to destroy the gods of the Canaanites (see Deut. 7:25-26).

Positively, the Israelites were to "observe my sabbaths" (v. 2), the second basic law. Basically that command referred to the weekly Sabbath observance to worship and acknowl-

edge God (Ex. 31:12-17). Recognizing God every seventh day
made the Israelites continually conscious of His involvement
in their total pattern of living. "This will be a sign between me
and you for the generations to come, so you may know that I
am the LORD, who makes you holy," God had said through
Moses when first instructing them to observe the Sabbath
(Ex. 31:13). The weekly celebration of the Sabbath would
continue to be "a sign between me and the Israelites forever"
(Ex. 31:17). Observing the Sabbath was their responsibility.
Making them holy was God's promise (Ex. 31:13).

The third command to be obeyed in maintaining the God-
Israel relationship was to "have reverence for my sanctuary"
(v. 2), a reminder that after bringing the Israelites out of
Egypt to be his people, God had commanded them to "make
a sanctuary for me, and I will dwell among them" (Ex. 25:8).
Many of the Israelites who heard the blessings and curses
presented in this chapter had participated in the building of
that sanctuary. They had witnessed the glory of God appear-
ing in the Tabernacle when it was dedicated (Lev. 9:23-24).
God had visibly filled the sanctuary with His presence, fulfilling His promise to dwell among them in the camp of Israel.

The Tabernacle was where the people met and worshiped
God. To the Tabernacle they brought their offerings in times
of thanksgiving as well as of repentance. In the Tabernacle
atonement was made for the sin of the nation, as the high
priest made intercession for them.

The Israelites were instructed to exercise utmost care and
reverence in approaching God. No unclean person was allowed to come to the sanctuary, but they were given extended
instructions (Lev. 11-15) for becoming clean so that they
could properly come into God's presence.

In contrast to the sanctuaries of the Canaanites, the Tabernacle in the camp of Israel was a holy place. Sacred prostitution, child sacrifice, and similar rites practiced in Canaanite
shrines had no place in Israel's holy place.

Divine blessings in material things and in God's presence
among them awaited the Israelites who responded obediently

to God's expectations after settling in Canaan. If they rejected idolatry, observed the Sabbath, and revered God's sanctuary as God's dwelling place among them, God promised to "walk among you and be your God" (vv. 3-13). God also promised them the providential care of seasonal rain to produce abundant crops from the fields and fruit from the trees. God would supply them with plenty of food to enjoy in safety (vv. 3-5).

"Peace in the land" was God's promise to the Israelites (vv. 6-8). Two aspects of that promise were of a very practical nature and would have been difficult for them to accomplish on their own. Abundant food supply would have been of limited value if they were threatened by wild beasts or invading armies. "I will remove savage beasts from the land" (v. 6) was God's promise to them. Numerous references indicate that lions and bears inhabited Canaan during Old Testament times (Judg. 14:8; 1 Sam. 17:34; 1 Kings 13:24-25; 2 Kings 2:24; 17:25-26; 1 Chron. 11:22).

"The sword will not pass through your country" (v. 6). Repeatedly in the days of the judges, surrounding nations oppressed the Israelites. Invading armies destroyed the crops, confiscated their animals, and occupied their pasture land (cf. Judg. 6:1-6). Palestine was the geographical bridge between the two great civilizations centered in the Nile and the Tigris-Euphrates valleys. Frequently the armies of ancient Egypt and Mesopotamia advanced through Palestine, subjecting the Israelites to the ravages of war (e.g., the Assyrians, c. 745-650 B.C., conquered Damascus and Samaria, threatened Jerusalem, and occupied Thebes in Egypt). God's promise provided protection during invasion and success in pursuing enemies even though the Israelites were greatly outnumbered.

The blessing promised to the Israelites in verses 9-13 is absolutely unique. No nation had a living, powerful deity residing among its people. But the Israelites had a living, omnipotent God dwelling among them and communicating with them. Note the comprehensive emphasis in these verses:

"I will look on you with favor . . .

> make you fruitful and increase your numbers . . .
> keep my covenant with you. . . .
> put my dwelling place among you and . . . not abhor you
> walk among you and be your God."

With words of comfort, God assured the Israelites that He would be gracious to them, increasing them in numbers and giving them bountiful material provisions. God would confirm His covenant, fulfilling all the promises made to Abraham. They had already been partially realized when He brought the Israelites out of Egyptian slavery, breaking "the bars of your yoke" and enabling them "to walk with your heads held high" (v. 13).

The uniqueness of God's presence with them had been the experience of the Israelites who received that assurance. They had seen God's glory in the pillar of cloud by day and a pillar of fire by night as they left Egypt (Ex. 13:21). His presence had been their protection when the Egyptians pursued them (Ex. 14:19-20). God's glory and presence had again been manifested when they grumbled against Him en route to Canaan, and God tested their obedience by supplying manna (Ex. 16:4, 7, 10). God's glory had again been manifested when the covenant between Himself and Israel was ratified on Mount Sinai (Ex. 24:16-17). The pillar of cloud had also hovered over Moses as God communicated through him with the Israelites (Ex. 33:9-10).

At the dedication of the Tabernacle God's glory had been manifested in a cloud covering, and His presence filled the sanctuary (Ex. 40:34). Then God's glory had appeared to the entire congregation of Israel and ignited the burnt offering (Lev. 9:6, 23), initiating the visible manifestation of His presence in the midst of the encampment.

All of those manifestations had been part of the experience of the Israelites. They had witnessed the manifestation of God's glory and had been made keenly aware of His awesome presence among them. Against that background, God promised to dwell among them when they entered Canaan.

"I will walk among you" (v. 12) should have been especially reassuring when they remembered God's relationship with those who had revered Him in times past. It was recorded that Enoch and Noah had walked with God (Gen. 5:22, 24; 6:9). Abraham and Isaac had walked before God (Gen. 17:1; 24:40; 48:15). Jacob had claimed that God as his Shepherd (Gen. 48:15) and had invoked His blessings on the sons of Joseph (Gen. 49). That God had used Moses to fulfill His promises to the patriarchs to free the Israelites from bondage (Ex. 3:6-10).

God reminded them that He had brought them out of bondage (v. 13). His continued walk with them confirmed that He would fulfill the rest of His promises and give them the land. Once they were in the land, God would continue to "walk among you" (v. 12).

The consequences of breaking the God-Israel relationship were spelled out in a series of curses (vv. 14-39). The curses were directly related to the attitude the Israelites would express toward God in their actions if they ignored and defied His instructions. They were warned that if they rejected the terms of the covenant those curses would come upon them.

Note the conditional nature of God's warnings:

"If you will not listen to me"
  "reject my decrees"
  "abhor my laws"
  "fail to carry out all my commands"
  "violate my covenant"

"Then . . . I will bring upon you . . . wasting diseases" and famine
  "set my face against you"

"If you will not listen to me"
Then "I will punish" (discipline)
  "break down your stubborn pride"
  "bring drought and crop failure"

"If you remain hostile toward me" (defy me)
  "refuse to listen to me"

Then "I will multiply your afflictions"
  "send wild animals against you" to rob and destroy
  "make you . . . few in number"

"If you continue to be hostile toward me"
"Then . . . I will be hostile" (with anger)
  "destroy your high places and altars"
  "abhor you"
  "lay waste the land and ruin cities"
  "reject your offerings"
  "scatter you among the nations"
  "make their hearts . . . fearful."

If they refused to listen and carry out God's instructions, they would violate the covenant and incur divine punishment. History shows that the nature of God's dealings with Israel was not one of sudden judgment. As He turned His face against her, He allowed the people to suffer illness, famine, and defeat. When they did not respond positively, God said, "I will punish [or, discipline] you." (The Hebrew word *yasar* used in verses 18 and 28 is best translated "to discipline, chasten, instruct." "From the usage and parallels in the OT, one must conclude that *yasar* and *musar* [discipline] denote correction which results in education."[1] Moses pointed out that God would discipline the Israelites "as a man disciplines his son" (Deut. 8:5; cf. Heb. 12:5-11).

The Israelites were warned that God would discipline them for their sins "seven times over" (vv. 18, 21, 24, 28). The use of the number *seven* is noteworthy. It appears also in the basic requirement to observe every seventh day as a Sabbath (27:2) and in the stipulation that in the religious year the seventh month was to be especially sacred. "Seven times over" was the judgment should they respond negatively to divine discipline.

Note how the hardship that was promised would intensify

---

1. Paul R. Gilchrist, "*yasar,*" in *Theological Wordbook of the Old Testament,* ed. R. Laird Harris; Gleason L. Archer, Jr.; Bruce K. Waltke (Chicago: Moody, 1980), p. 386.

if they continued to be hostile toward God. They would suffer drought, bad crops, and wild animals. War, plagues, famine, cannibalism, and devastation would overtake them. Finally, they would be deported from the land to suffer in exile.

God's feelings toward His people would also intensify as they defied Him. "I will set my face against you" (v. 17). "I myself . . . in my anger I will be hostile" (vv. 24, 28). "I will abhor you" (v. 30). "I will scatter you among the nations and will draw out my sword and pursue you" (v. 33).

When exile became a reality, God's word for "those of you who are left" was, "I will make their hearts so fearful . . ." that they will be insecure, terrified by the slightest threat. Bearing their own guilt and that of their forefathers, they would perish among the nations, be devoured by their enemies, and waste away.

Confession of sin is the way back to God (vv. 40-45). Even when the nation was in exile and suffering divine discipline, there was, for those who were willing to confess their and their forefathers' defiance and hostility toward God, hope of restoring their relationship with God. When they had been humbled, suffering for the sin of rejecting God's decrees, then God would respond. "For their sake" (those who confessed their sin), God would remember His covenant with their ancestors whom He had brought out of Egypt.

God spoke of the time when "uncircumcised hearts [would be] humbled" (v. 41). Physical circumcision was a sign of the covenant (Gen. 17:10-12), required of Israelites as well as aliens who wished to participate in the Passover (Ex. 12:48-49). In exhorting the Israelites to love God wholeheartedly, Moses admonished them, "Circumcise your hearts, therefore, and do not be stiff-necked any longer" (Deut. 10:16). He assured them that if they returned to God in obedience, He would restore them to their land and "circumcise your hearts . . . so that you may love him with all your heart" (Deut. 30:6). In spiritual circumcision, everything that interfered with their vital relationship with God had to be removed.

Consider how the ultimate condition of the Israelites, suffering in exile, is related to the requirements for maintaining a vital relationship with God (26:1-2). Instead of destroying the idols as God had commanded (Deut. 7) they had embraced idolatry. Because they had turned to idols, God would "destroy your high places, cut down your incense altars and pile your dead bodies on the lifeless forms of your idols, and I will abhor you" (26:30).

Idolatry had disrupted their observance of the Sabbaths. How could they acknowledge God in thanksgiving on the weekly Sabbath and in the festivals throughtout the year when they were serving idols? Thrust out of the land that God had given them, they could not enjoy the harvests and crops that He provided for them. Consequently the land would lie waste and "enjoy its sabbath years" (vv. 31-35). The Sabbaths they had failed to observe (25:4) would be observed while they were in exile. Years later Jeremiah repeated that prediction (25:11), and it was fulfilled (2 Chron. 36:21).

Neither could the Israelites reverence God's sanctuary while they were in exile. God had promised them that He would dwell with them in their camp and among them in the land that He would give them. Turning to idolatry and worshiping at pagan shrines would be a failure to revere God's sanctuary among them. In Israel's subsequent history God abandoned His sanctuary among the people, as was vividly portrayed in Ezekiel's vision (Ezek. 8-11), which was followed by the Temple and Jerusalem's being abandoned to the Babylonians for destruction.

VOWS AND DEDICATIONS (27:1-34)

The book of Leviticus concluded with a consideration of vows that voluntarily placed persons or property in a special, consecrated relationship with God. Whereas the opening chapters prescribed the offerings that the congregation of Israel and individual Israelites must offer at the sanctuary, this chapter deals with voluntary offerings and vows (27:1-34).

Vows are expressions of piety, religious pledges. They are transactions between man and God, in which one dedicates himself, his service, or something valuable to God. Vows are self-imposed and often made in the context of self-discipline, with a view to accomplishing certain goals in one's relationship with God.

Vows, or promises, to God were voluntary, not required under the law (Deut. 23:21-23). However, if vows were made, they were to be fulfilled. Rash vows were to be avoided (Prov. 20:25; Eccl. 5:4-5). A Nazirite vow, in which a person committed himself to abstinence, consecration, and dedication to the Lord, usually held for a specified period of time (Num. 6:1-21). Vows that involved others, especially in a family or marital relationship, could be nullified (Num. 30:1-16).

Leviticus 27 gives instructions for vows of persons (vv. 1-8), animals (vv. 9-13), property (vv. 14-29), and produce (vv. 30-34).

A person's being dedicated to the service of God at the sanctuary was the most basic vow (vv. 2-8). As a personal commitment, it was made on an individual basis. Since individuals as young as one month could be dedicated (v. 6), parents must have been held responsible for vows involving children.

The passage gives few details as to how the vows were carried out practically. Since the Levites had been assigned the care of the Tabernacle, it hardly seems likely that all who might feel prompted to make such vows would actually have opportunity to work there. Certainly children as young as one month would not have been able to serve until they were older.

Such dedication was given a monetary value so that those vows could be fulfilled by paying the symbolic equivalent of service into the Tabernacle treasury. The monetary value seems to be related to the price of a slave. Exodus 21:32 names the price of a slave as thirty shekels, although it probably varied widely. (For example, as a teenager Joseph was sold for twenty shekels [Gen. 37:1, 28].) Here in Leviticus, the

value ranges from three to fifty shekels according to the age
and sex of the individual involved. If one was unable to pay,
the priest would set an affordable price. Thus any person
making a vow could discharge of his own free will the obligation he had incurred.

A person might feel prompted to make a vow in which he
promised an animal to God (vv. 9-13). That may have occurred quite frequently; the instructions for bringing
fellowship offerings provided for it (Lev. 7:16; 22:18-23; cf.
Deut. 12:11, 17).

If a clean animal was offered in a vow, it was declared holy
and acceptable for sacrifice. Once designated as an offering
to fulfill a vow, no substitution of species or quality could be
made.

If an unclean animal was promised, it was to be presented
to the priest for evaluation. It could then be sold at a fixed
price, or the owner could purchase it back (redeem it) at the
stated price plus twenty percent, and the proceeds would be
given to the sanctuary.

When land was dedicated in a vow, the time remaining until
the year of jubilee had to be considered (vv. 16-25). The price
was fixed according to the size of the field and the number of
years remaining, with a shekel for each homer (about six
bushels) of barley per year. The owner could repurchase the
land by adding twenty percent to the established price. If he
did not redeem it and it was sold, then he could not reclaim it.
In the year of jubilee it would become the perpetual property
of the priests. If a person dedicated land he had purchased,
then he had to pay the determined value annually until the
year of jubilee, when it would revert to the original owner.

Excluded from dedicatory vows were the firstborn of
animals (vv. 26-27), since they already belonged to God (cf.
Ex. 12:13; 13:12; 34:20; Num. 18:15). But the firstborn of
unclean animals could be sold or redeemed and the proceeds
given to the sanctuary.

Excluded from being able to be ransomed were proscribed
things or whatever had been irrevocably devoted to the Lord,

whether man, animal, or property (vv. 28-29). The Hebrew word *hērem,* "devoted thing," or "ban," basically meant "the exclusion of an object from the use or abuse of man and its irrevocable surrender to God."[2] Consequently any man, animal, or property that had been devoted to the Lord was holy and could not be sold or redeemed by substituting something else; the owner had no claim to it. It could, however, be given to the priest for the support of religious ceremonies (cf. Num. 18:14; Josh. 6:19).

Actually, the verb form of *hērem* "usually . . . means a ban for utter destruction, the compulsory dedication of something which impedes or resists God's work, which is considered to be accursed before God."[3] The Israelites made such a vow before they fought with the Canaanites (Num. 21:2-3). They promised that if God would give them victory, they would not retain any spoil of war for themselves but devote everything to God for utter destruction. (Note also the cities totally destroyed under Joshua [Josh. 6:21; 8:26; 10:28; 11:11].)

"No person devoted to destruction may be ransomed; he must be put to death" (v. 29). Consider God's command to the Israelites to destroy utterly the idolators with their idols and their idolatrous shrines, which were detestable to God (Deut. 7:1-5, 26). They could not be dedicated in a vow to God for service.

Moses enlarged on this later, when he addressed the Israelites before his death. Anyone who encouraged the worship of other gods and preached rebellion against the God who had brought the Israelites out of Egypt was to be stoned (Deut. 13:1-11). Even the city that tolerated such rebellious idolatry was to be utterly destroyed (Deut. 13:12-18). Consequently, in making vows they were warned that idolatrous

---

2. Leon J. Wood, *"haram,"* in *Theological Wordbook of the Old Testament,* ed. R. Laird Harris; Gleason L. Archer, Jr.; Bruce K. Waltke (Chicago: Moody, 1980), p. 324.
3. Ibid.

people condemned to destruction were not to be ransomed.

By contrast, the Israelites were God's holy people (Deut. 7:6). God had demonstrated His love for Israel in redeeming her from Egyptian bondage. He had assured her that He would keep "his covenant of love to a thousand generations of those who love him and keep his commands" (Deut. 7:9).

"But those who hate him he will repay to their face by destruction; he will not be slow to repay to their face those who hate him" (Deut. 7:10). In those words the Israelites were warned that divine judgment would be upon them if they hated God, who had admonished them to listen to His commands.

Assuring the Israelites of His continued love and blessing (Deut. 7:12-16), God promised them that He would release His power, as He had done in Egypt, to aid them in destroying Canaan's idolatrous culture (Deut. 7:17-26).

The tithe was also excluded from any vows the Israelites made (vv. 30-34). Since God was the owner of the land given to them in Canaan, the Israelites were expected, as tenants, to give one-tenth of their produce to God (Lev. 25:23). If a landowner decided to redeem a tithe, he had to pay a twenty percent premium.

Every tenth animal from the herd and flock also belonged to God. To avoid arbitrary selection, the Israelites were instructed to take every tenth animal that passed under the shepherd's rod and offer that animal to God. If the owner attempted to make a substitute, then both animals were appropriated for the sanctuary.

Abraham was the first person identified as giving a tithe (Gen. 14:20). Later Jacob made a vow to give one-tenth of his possessions to God if he were divinely prospered (Gen. 28:20-22). When Aaron and his sons were appointed as priests, the Levites were assigned the responsibility of caring for the Tabernacle and were given no territory in Canaan, so the rest of the Israelites were instructed to bring tithes to the sanctuary to be given to the Levites (Num. 18:21-32).

Deuteronomy records further instructions for the giving of

the tithe. Bringing it to the central sanctuary, the Israelites were to rejoice (12:7, 11-12, 18; 14:22-26) with the Levites and priests. Through bringing their tithes in joyful worship at the sanctuary, they would "learn to revere the LORD [their] God always" (Deut. 14:23). If it were done in sincerity, the Israelites would have an annual reminder that they were stewards, tenants accountable to God, who had entrusted them with the land.

Vows were voluntary; anything an Israelite wanted to dedicate to God through a vow was beyond what was legally required. Once a vow was made, however, it was not to be treated lightly. Consequently the legislation of chapter 27 was designed to discourage impulsive acts and hastily made promises lest anyone profane God's holiness. Under certain conditions that which was vowed could be redeemed.

SELECT BIBLIOGRAPHY

Bonar, Andrew A. *A Commentary on the Book of Leviticus.* 1851. Reprint. Grand Rapids: Zondervan, 1959.

Craigie, Peter C. *The Book of Deuteronomy.* Grand Rapids: Eerdmans, 1976.

Douglas, M. *Purity and Danger.* Rev. ed. London: Routledge & Kegan Paul, 1978.

Guthrie, Donald, ed. *The New Bible Commentary: Revised.* Grand Rapids: Eerdmans, 1970.

Harris, R. Laird; Archer, Gleason L., Jr.; and Waltke, Bruce K., eds. *Theological Wordbook of the Old Testament.* 2 vols. Chicago: Moody, 1980.

Harrison, R. K. *Leviticus.* Downers Grove, Ill.: Inter-Varsity, 1980.

―――. "Leviticus." In *Introduction to the Old Testament.* Grand Rapids: Eerdmans, 1969.

Keil, C. F. *Biblical Commentary on the Old Testament,* Vol. 2, *The Pentateuch.* Reprint. Grand Rapids: Eerdmans, 1949.

Kellogg, S. H. *The Book of Leviticus.* London: Hodder & Stoughton, 1899.

Schultz, Samuel J. *The Old Testament Speaks.* 3d ed. New York: Harper & Row, 1980.

―――. *The Gospel of Moses.* Chicago: Moody, 1975.

Wenham, Gordon J. *The Book of Leviticus.* Grand Rapids: Eerdmans, 1979.

Moody Press, a ministry of the Moody Bible Institute, is designed for education, evangelization, and edification. If we may assist you in knowing more about Christ and the Christian life, please write us without obligation: Moody Press, c/o MLM, Chicago, Illinois 60610.